A Bintel Brief

D0024220

A Bintel Brief

SIXTY YEARS OF LETTERS FROM THE LOWER EAST SIDE TO THE *JEWISH DAILY FORWARD*

❖ ❖ ❖

COMPILED, EDITED AND
WITH AN INTRODUCTION
by Isaac Metzker

FOREWORD AND NOTES
by Harry Golden

BEHRMAN HOUSE INC., PUBLISHERS
NEW YORK, NEW YORK

The Lower East Side photographic portfolio in this book has been provided through the courtesy of the Jewish Museum, New York, New York

PHOTO CREDITS FOR ILLUSTRATIONS
FOLLOWING PAGES 72 AND 144

1) Lewis W. Hine, George Eastman House, Rochester, New York
2) Edwin Levick, Library of Congress, Washington, D.C.
3) Lewis W. Hine, George Eastman House, Rochester, New York
4) Lewis W. Hine, George Eastman House, Rochester, New York
5) Uknown photographer, Library of Congress, Washington, D.C.
6) Lewis W. Hine, George Eastman House, Rochester, New York
7) Unknown photographer, Library of Congress, Washington, D.C.
8) Alice Austen, Alice Austen Collection, Staten Island Historical Society
9) Jessie Tarbox Beals, Community Service Society, New York, New York
10) Lewis W. Hine, George Eastman House, Rochester, New York
11) Jacob A. Riis, The Jacob A. Riis Collection, The Museum of the City of New York
12) Lewis W. Hine, National Committee on Employment of Youth, New York, New York
13) Lewis W. Hine, George Eastman House, Rochester, New York
14) Lewis W. Hine, George Eastman House, Rochester, New York
15) Lewis W. Hine, National Committee on Employment of Youth, New York, New York
16) Lewis W. Hine, George Eastman House, Rochester, New York
17) Lewis W. Hine, National Committee on Employment of Youth, New York, New York
18) Unknown photographer, International Ladies Garment Workers Union
19) Unknown photographer, Amalgamated Clothing Workers of America

Published in association with the Black Star Publishing Company

Translation and Introduction Copyright © 1971 by Isaac Metzker
Foreword and Notes Copyright © 1971 by Doubleday & Company, Inc.
All Rights Reserved
Printed in the United States of America

Library of Congress Cataloging in Publication Data
Main entry under title:

A Bintel brief.

Reprint. Originally published: Garden City,
N. Y.: Doubleday, 1971.
Includes index.
1. Jews—New York (City)—Social life and
customs. 2. New York (City)—Social life and
customs. I. Metzker, Isaac, 1902–
II. Forverts.
F128.9.J5B46 1982   974.7'1004924   82-12941
ISBN 0-87441-345-1

1982 edition published by Behrman House, Inc. Publishers
1261 Broadway, New York, New York 10001

"A Bintel Brief" was translated by Diana Shalet Levy.

I wish to express my gratitude to my wife, Bella S. Metzker, for assisting in the translation, for helping me with the revision and corrections of the manuscript.

I.M.

Introduction

In 1880 when America had a population of fifty million, one quarter of a million of that total were Jews. The majority of these Jews were German and Sephardic who had come here with the languages of the countries in which their families had lived for generations. The new immigrants whose mother tongue was Yiddish were at that time in the minority.

The mass immigration of the Yiddish-speaking Jews from Eastern Europe started in the early 1880s. They were fleeing from the bloody pogroms in Russia and Rumania and from poverty and persecution in other Eastern European countries.

The mass immigration of Jews to the United States was like the wandering of peoples in ancient times and it seemed for a time that some of the Eastern European countries would be completely drained of their Jewish populations. The situation might possibly have come to that point, in fact, had it not been for the passage of strict quota laws at the beginning of the 1920s which all but closed the gates of America to these immigrants.

From 1881 to 1925, however, 2,650,000 Jewish immigrants managed to come to America from Eastern European countries alone. At that time this total amounted to a third of the Jewish population of all of Eastern Europe.

Wonderful tales had come from remote America to the Jews in Eastern Europe, even to the most far-flung towns and villages where no railways ran. Such magic words as "Golden Land," "Freedom," "Equality," had animated them—somewhere, across the great ocean, a new land was being built, founded on freedom and equality for all people, a refuge for all who were suffering and persecuted.

For the impoverished and tormented Jews, these tales seemed

the fulfillment of their dreams of finding a haven for themselves and their families, a place somewhere under the sun where they could have peace and live like human beings. These dreams and the tales they heard gave them the courage to set out for this country on the long quest for freedom and bread. They plodded along Europe's paths and roads, stole across borders in the dark of night, traveled by horse and wagon and train, endured a long painful voyage across the stormy ocean.

On the American shore, near Ellis Island, the Goddess of Freedom held high the bright torch for the immigrants. She enticed them with promises and stimulated their imagination. Many of them believed that as soon as they disembarked from the boat they would find heaven on earth and an end to all their suffering. But they were to experience many bitter disappointments in the new land.

In those years when new Jewish immigrants were arriving daily from Eastern Europe, committees were formed among the Jews already settled to encourage the newcomers to go west. But a great many of them preferred to remain near the shore where they had left the ship. They settled in the old tenements of New York, primarily in a small area of the Lower East Side. There, crowded together, they stayed near *landsleit* who had migrated before them, or near friends who had come on the same boat.

It did not take them long to find out that no luxuries awaited them—that one had to struggle hard here for the necessities of life. The transition from their old way of life in the *shtetel* to a new life in the seething, vast city of New York was not an easy one to make. Back home, everything had been founded on traditional Judaism. There the Sabbath was sacred. Even an unbeliever would not dare desecrate the Sabbath in public. *Kashruth* was carefully observed; the Jewish holidays were properly celebrated. Even few "enlightened" men in small towns would dare to trim or shave their beards.

Thus had the Jews conducted themselves within strong traditions for generations and generations. Now, suddenly, they were thrust into a totally different world where they found it necessary to break with tradition and flout time-honored laws. They went to work on the Sabbath, they shaved their beards, and many of them began to eat non-*kosher* foods.

The "green" years were difficult and full of problems for the immigrants. Thousands and thousands of them were drawn into the needle trades and many found other types of employment. Working men and women at that time were not yet organized, and the majority of them were terribly exploited by their bosses. These were the days of the real "sweatshop" system. Not only the adults but children too worked under the worst conceivable conditions . . . often seven days a week, twelve and even fourteen hours a day, and for miserable wages. The immigrants lived in poverty, crowded in small damp rooms without daylight or fresh air. In the summer it was hard to breathe in the tenements and during the stifling nights they often slept by the thousands on the roofs.

Not only did they usually work for meager wages, but during slack times there were no jobs at any wage. Unemployment lasted for long periods of time. The immigrants often lacked the money to make the all-important payment on a steamship ticket purchased on the installment plan for someone else in the family waiting to immigrate. There was no bread, milk or money for rent.

During depression periods it was not uncommon to see families huddled on the sidewalks with their meager household effects. They had been thrown out of their apartments by the landlords because they were behind in their rent payments. Often, a plate was placed for collecting rent money near a haggard mother who sat with her little children on their bedding. Neighbors and passers-by who were moved by the scene threw coins in the dish. A few dollars might accumulate by the end of the day, and toward evening a neighbor would take the small sum to the landlord, who would let the family back into their apartment.

In those years of mass immigration there was much to be deplored in this country, most specifically in the great city of New York. Countless wrongs were committed against the new immigrants, many of which even violated the principles of the

United States Constitution. The poverty was oppressive, and more than one newcomer was driven to suicide.

Nevertheless, the majority of the immigrants refused to give up their dreams. They would not, they could not. The visions that had accompanied them to the new land persisted.

Within them raged a protest against all that was evil here but they seemed to sense a promised freedom in the air and did not lose faith. They still believed that things could be good for them in the "Golden Land" and spoke with assurance about the good life awaiting their children. They knew that they had not come here as invaders, forcing their way into a country already built up and populated by a people for generations. And their awareness that they had come with the same rights as the many other immigrants of various nationalities who had settled here and begun to build a new, richer life bolstered their courage. They were young and energetic and would not be easily discouraged. They were determined to make this country their home.

The *Forward*, a Yiddish daily newspaper in America which celebrated its seventieth anniversary in 1967, played an important role in helping the Eastern European Jewish immigrants transplant and adjust themselves to American life.

Many of the immigrants had grown up in remote areas where a newspaper was seldom seen. But here in the new land, when they saw a newspaper with the familiar *Alef-Beis* that they had known from the Prayer Book, the Pentateuch, or from their mothers' "Ladies' Bible," they were drawn to the publication. It was as if their *Alef-Beis* from home and *kheyder* had followed them to America. And when they took the Yiddish newspaper in their hands and found that they could read it, they were pleasantly surprised. The eye first caught a headline printed in large letters about an important news item. But with the reading came increased appetite and little by little they plunged into the density of the small print.

There were some among these new arrivals who, back in the

old country, *had* read a newspaper, a Yiddish periodical, a brochure on Socialism, Zionism, or something of Jewish literature. Among these there were some who had the potential to become leaders and educators in the social and cultural life of the immigrants.

The *Jewish Daily Forward*, which was primarily a workingman's newspaper, attracted many of the immigrants who had become shopworkers. The paper began to teach them about trade unionism. It explained in their mother tongue how important it was for them to be organized, to unite to fight for higher wages, shorter working hours and decent treatment by the bosses. And the newcomers, who were lonely here, clung to the *Forward* in turn as to a newfound friend. It became their teacher and guide. The newspaper concerned itself with their lot, spoke to their hearts and quickly gained their respect and confidence.

It is no exaggeration to say that the pages of the *Forward* over the seven decades contain a true epical history of the Jewish mass immigration and the immigrants' adaptation to life in this country. The saga of their struggles, achievements and contributions to the country were written into the day-by-day news. All sorts of articles, literary novels, sketches and special features were printed in this newspaper.

One of these features in the *Forward* was and still is the "Bintel Brief."

Abraham Cahan was, except for a brief interval, the editor of the newspaper from its founding until shortly before his death in 1951. He maintained that the *Forward* should not devote itself exclusively to trade unionism, to political and social problems. From the outset, he broadened the interests of the paper and enlivened it with varied reading material, including light articles dealing with daily life. The daily newspaper thus drew readers from all strata and classes.

The popularity and circulation of the *Forward* grew at a rapid pace. It became the biggest, most influential Yiddish newspaper in America. By the early thirties the paper could boast of a circulation of a quarter of a million.

With its wide coverage and the important material it printed, the newspaper exercised a tremendous influence on Jewish life in America.

Mr. Cahan, who became well known as a talented author with his novel, *The Rise of David Levinsky*, and other works, was a strong advocate of realism. He not only printed realistic stories by well-known writers but made an effort to bring the reality of Jewish life in America into his newspaper. Through light articles he inspired and encouraged the readers to write to the *Forward* about any unusual events in their own lives, and about their own problems. Mr. Cahan firmly believed that "truth is stranger than fiction," and as far back as 1903 planned a special feature for the newspaper in which the readers could express themselves, a section of the paper which would mirror real life. As a result, the daily feature, "A Bintel Brief," was established in 1906. It immediately became very popular and is still, to this day, a most important feature of the paper.

The first three letters were printed with an introduction by the editor on January 20, 1906. One of the letters, written by a woman, gives us an insight into the poverty in which the immigrant working-class families lived on the Lower East Side. The woman had a sick husband, and their eldest son was the bread-winner of the family. The son wanted very much to own a watch and chain, the sort that were then being worn across the front of the vest. For a long time he saved from his lunch money until he was able to buy himself the watch. But it seems the watch lay hidden in the dresser most of the time and, according to the woman's letter, it became their security against poverty. Since they could never save a dollar and lived from hand to mouth, every time "slack season" came, she took the watch to the pawnshop. For the few dollars she got there, they were able to live through a period in which there was no work.

Suddenly the watch disappeared. Her son was unemployed and she wanted to take the watch to the pawnshop but couldn't find it. She suspected that a poor neighbor of hers, who came to the house quite often and was also jobless, had been driven by her own need to take her son's watch to pawn. Since it was embarrassing to discuss the matter personally with the neighbor, the woman appealed to her through the *Forward* to send her the pawn ticket in the mail. She assured her neighbor, in the letter, that she would never reproach her because she knew her condition only too well, and added that they would remain friends.

The feature, "A Bintel Brief," caught on quickly. For many readers the letters awakened a desire to unburden their hearts, to reveal their own problems and ask for advice. Whole sacks of mail began to pour in. Often the daily column contained several letters.

Abraham Cahan wrote in his memoirs (1929) the following about the "Bintel Brief":

"People often need the opportunity to be able to pour out their heavy-laden hearts. Among our immigrant masses this need was very marked. Hundreds of thousands of people, torn from their homes and their dear ones, were lonely souls who thirsted for expression, who wanted to hear an opinion, who wanted advice in solving their weighty problems. The 'Bintel Brief' created just this opportunity for them.

"Many of the letters we receive are poorly written and we must correct or rewrite them. Some of the letters are not written directly by the people who seek the advice, but by others who do it for them. It has even become a special occupation for certain people to write letters for those who cannot write. There also appeared small signs with the inscription 'Here letters are written to the "Bintel Brief."' [The price for writing such a letter ranged from twenty-five to fifty cents. I.M.] Often the professional 'Bintel Brief' writer let himself go with his own eloquence, but this, naturally, was deleted. And from time to time men and women came to the editorial office to ask that someone write a letter for them about their problems.

"Through the 'Bintel Brief' mothers have found the children they had lost many years ago. One mother, who had lost her child when it was an infant, found it through the 'Bintel Brief' some twenty years later. Such cases occurred countless times in the twenty-three years since the feature was first established.

"The name of the feature, 'Bintel Brief,' became so popular that it is often used as a part of American Yiddish. When we speak of an interesting event in family life, you can hear a comment like 'A remarkable story—just for the "Bintel Brief."' Other times you can hear, 'It's like a "Bintel Brief" story!' Many of the themes from the letters have been used by writers of dramas and sketches for their works, because a world of literary import can be found in them.

"The first few years I used to answer all the letters myself. I did it with the greatest pleasure, because in the letters one sees a rare panorama of human souls and because I also had a literary interest in the work."

During the sixty-five years of this daily feature, tens of thousands of letters have been printed. A great many of them mirror not only the varied problems of Jewish immigrant life in America but also the earth-shaking and catastrophic world events of this period.

One finds in the "Bintel Brief" many short biographies of people who barely escaped with their lives from disasters that raged like hurricanes over their heads and homes. The immigrants had numerous problems when they emerged from the turmoil of World War I, the Russian Revolution, the rise of Communism, and the Nazi German holocaust.

As one leafs through the pages of over sixty years of the "Bintel Brief," one sees the themes changing with the passage of time. Old problems vanish and new ones appear. One also notices that the mood and approach to certain problems change. Over-all social progress, improved working conditions, state and federal reforms, and an increasingly higher standard of living solved many of the problems which they had to cope with.

It would seem incredible to a present-day reader to read in the "Bintel Brief" column, for example, a protest letter printed in 1906 about the actions of a boss. This particular letter de-

nounced the boss for deducting two cents from the wages of a
thirteen-year-old worker who earned two and a half dollars a
week, simply because he came to work ten minutes late.

Today's young Jewish-American mothers would think it was a
contrived story if they were told that many years ago poor women
of the East Side, who might have been their own grandmothers,
wrote to the "Bintel Brief" pleading that someone take their
children for adoption because they could not bear watching them
go hungry.

The problems contained in the letters to the "Bintel Brief"
were varied. Almost all of the readers of and the letter writers
to the *Forward* in the early days were young, newly arrived immigrants. And what did they not write about in those days! The
letters can be divided into categories: trivial, serious, comic and
tragic. All of them, even the tritest and most sentimental, can
serve as a sociological study of the people, of their environment,
and of the times in which they lived.

Many of the letters at that time dealt with love and jealousy,
with whether to marry or not, with love affairs between boarders
and the married women in whose homes they lived.

The most tragic letters of those early years were written about
poverty, unemployment and starvation, about young people in
the sweatshops developing tuberculosis, about young girls lured
into brothels. A great many pathetic, touching letters were printed
from despairing women whose husbands had deserted them and
their children, leaving them with no means of support. The
women appealed to their husbands through the "Bintel Brief,"
pleading with them to have pity and return home to their starving
children.

The number of men who left their families became so great
at one time that the *Forward* with the help of the National
Desertion Bureau established a special column to trace them. In
this column, which was titled "The Gallery of Missing Husbands,"
they printed the pictures of the men and many of them were
found.

As time went on, the subject matter of the letters changed and continued to change a great deal.

The majority of the present-day letter writers have now been in the country for many years, and they are no longer young. Many of them are now retired; they are well established here, with children and grandchildren. The problems they now write about to the "Bintel Brief" deal mainly with family matters. Mothers-in-law complain about their daughters-in-law; daughters-in-law complain about their mothers-in-law; a mother is concerned that her twenty-two-year-old daughter is in no hurry to get married; an old father, disappointed in his children, wants to bequeath his fortune to charity; a grandmother disowns her only grandson because he married a Gentile girl; a woman complains because her husband, already past seventy, is carrying on a love affair with a young widow.

Many of the letter writers today are old readers of the *Forward* and their close ties to the newspaper, as well as their confidence in the editor of the "Bintel Brief," have grown stronger and deeper over the years. They often express their trust with an opening remark like: "You are the only one whom I can trust and to whom I can pour out my heart . . ." "As a reader of the *Forverts* since 1910, when the big cloakmakers' strike took place, I appeal to you for advice, and I will do as you tell me . . ." "I know that no one can advise me as well as you can." One reader writes that his asking for an opinion and counsel from the editor reminds him of the way people went to the *rebbe* in the old country.

The editor who answers the letters is far removed from the role of the *rebbe* (who gave people not only advice but blessings and amulets too). But, in his answers to the letters, the editor is more than just an adviser who gives perfunctory counsel. He is also the teacher and the preacher, and often his answer to a letter turns into an instructive lecture.

In this book, A BINTEL BRIEF, I have shortened or condensed some of the letters and most of the editor's answers. In some of the answers I have given only a synopsis covering the essence of the editor's reply.

In selecting the letters my purpose was to choose those which depict the true story of the immigrants, uprooted from the Old World, who came here determined to build a new life.

The letters are arranged in chronological order and the year each appeared in the *Forward* is noted.

Isaac Metzker

Foreword

The "Bintel Brief" (letters to the editor) is indeed a concise and poignant history of the way the immigrant Jews fitted into their new adopted home, America. Abe Cahan, the novelist and the great editor of the *Jewish Daily Forward*, started the "Bintel Brief" in 1906 after realizing from some letters the paper received that there was a need to respond on a regular basis to readers' problems that were well beyond the realm of the lovesick.

Letters from hundreds of immigrant Jews inundated the editorial desk. They asked for advice on many subjects. Leon Gottleib, then Mr. Cahan's editorial assistant, spoke to him about the amount of daily mail. In particular, he wondered about three letters that he could not place in any of the paper's existing departments.

Thus the "Bintel Brief's" initiation. Here were some of the early questions:

"I am a Socialist and my boss is a fine man. I know he's a Capitalist but I like him. Am I doing something wrong?"

"I am a Socialist and going with an American girl. She wants to go to dances and balls and affairs and I would like to know if you think it is all right for me to go, too."

"My son is already twenty-six years old and doesn't want to get married. He says he is a Socialist and he is too busy. Socialism is Socialism but getting married is important, too."

"My son was against my marriage but I have left my second husband and I am getting a divorce. My son reads the *For-*

ward and I plead with him to forgive me. I am as lonely as a stone."

"My husband reads the *Forward,* but where does he read it? In the barbershop where he goes all the time with those other card players. Let him see this letter."

"Is it a sin to use face powder? Shouldn't a girl look beautiful? My father does not want me to use face powder. Is it a sin?"

It is true that Abe Cahan always favored the human interest story. In one of his early light articles, he wrote about the Italian barber who fell in love with a Jewish girl on Broome Street. He wanted to marry her, but her mother wouldn't bless the match. Finally the mother agreed to the marriage provided the barber converted to Judaism. The mother made the new husband learn Hebrew and he had to pray every morning wearing his *yarmulka.* The Italian and his Jewish wife lived with the mother, and the barber did not get his breakfast until he had prayed. But that wasn't all. The wife had a brother named Joe and Joe never prayed before breakfast. So the barber asked his mother-in-law what was the difference between him and the brother? The answer was, "Joe's a Jew. I know he's a Jew but you've got to prove you're one."

Between the years 1899 and 1914 more than one and a half million European Jews came to the United States. This represents the second highest influx of immigrants during this period, the Italians taking first place.

The disastrous Russo-Japanese war had brought the high point of the persecution of the Jews in Russia. It led to the fearful pogrom in Kishinev on Easter 1903 in which forty-five Jews were killed, many thousands wounded and a large number of women raped. Almost 1500 Jewish shops and houses were destroyed and most of the synagogues were looted. But the year of the harshest village raids by the Cossacks, 1906, was the high point of the Jewish departure from Europe for these shores.

The total Jewish immigration from 1899 to the beginning of World War I in 1914 was 1,532,690.

Most of the immigrants arrived in the United States in relative poverty, only some 7 per cent having as much as fifty dollars in their pockets. More than half had no money at all—their capital was hope.

More than other immigrant groups, a large proportion of the Jews brought their women and children along. There were forty-four Jewish women to every fifty-six Jewish men; and twenty-four children under fourteen to every seventy-six adults. And nearly 70 per cent of these families had paid their passage with money borrowed from relatives.

The pattern was fairly standard. The Jewish fathers and brothers came to America first and worked to earn enough for a *shiff's carte* (steamship passage). They then brought their wives and children over. More than a million Jewish women and children followed husbands and fathers to the New World, more women and children than of any other immigrant group.

From 1914 to 1920, that is, during World War I and its immediate aftermath, Jewish immigration to the United States virtually closed. But after the war the wave increased once again (more than 120,000 in 1921 alone), until the new immigration laws went into effect in 1922, when the total number dropped to less than half of what it had been previous years.

Some of these immigrants to America pushed on to the Midwest or the South or New England. But most of them stopped in New York City, settling in the district known as the Lower East Side. This entire area was composed of ghettos within the larger ghetto. The sections along the East River were populated by Italians, while the Irish took over the blocks facing the Hudson. When the Italians began to spill into the Jewish quarter, the Jews moved out. As soon as the Williamsburg Bridge spanned the two boroughs, thousands of Jews moved over into the Williamsburg section of Brooklyn.

Scattered throughout the Lower East Side were small enclaves of Poles, whom we had always heard were the original anti-Semites of Europe. Funny how the Poles, who had the entire American continent to drift about, settled cheek to jowl with Jewish immigrants.

Talk about integration! The Jewish households in those days set up no barriers between the young and old, the poor and the well to do, the misfit and the conformist. They all lived together, if not in harmony, then at least in a sense of common participation in the vitality of their district and that era. Today we have the old who often wonder how to spend empty years, and we have an entire new government-sponsored social science called geriatrics which tries to guide us in the proper disposition of the American aged. And of course we have the poor in another category and the radicals, the intellectuals, the hard hats, the law and order boys and God knows who else, each in their own compartments, as American life grows more segregated and we all approach an unfortunate condition of ultimate polarization. In the ghettos of New York, the crotchety maiden aunt, Grandmother and Grandfather, the wild-eyed high school boy who had just begun to study Marx, Uncle Boris from uptown and the boarder who studied Spinoza and Shakespeare until late at night every night—all sat at the same table and shared the same bread, soup and potatoes. They also got involved in many-sided conversations and debates. Today we have TV by satellite and two-way wrist-watch radios right out of the Dick Tracy comic strip, but we communicate very poorly if at all between poor and rich, youth and oldster, radical and conservative.

All things considered, and there were some very bad times, make no mistake, I think we were lucky to grow up in that period of immigrant America; we were happier, perhaps, than the kids are today with their two-hundred-dollar mini-bikes, the most expensive toys ever pushed onto an unsuspecting generation of suburban parents. If nothing else, we had an atmosphere of vitality and excitement. The air swarmed with the smell of used clothing, dung in the ghettos and salamis hanging in the shops—but it was bracing to a man's nostrils and free at least of smog, carbon monoxide and the fumes from chemical plants.

Anyway, the Jews had the sure cure for the doldrums, the blues, the fits of melancholia and depression that seem to plague the middle class today, and that was humor. In all my years on the Lower East Side I never saw anybody take a tranquilizer or a sleeping pill—not one! But I heard jokes and wisecracks all day long from the breakfast table until late at night. Looking back, I still feel that given almost everyone's circumstances this was a great wonder—the puns, the poke in the ribs, the teasing, the ribbing and the smiles and outright howls of laughter. Even for the disease that afflicted so many of them they had a comic name; tuberculosis was "Jewish asthma." And even anti-Semitism was answered with humor, as the Jews saw the absurdity of the hatemongers pretending to possess logic and sanity. The immigrant Jews saw humor in their own situation, too, in the fierce struggle to Americanize, to be like the tall blond confident native citizens. They joked about Talmudic commentators ("I wonder what Raschi would say about that?"). Ghetto humor was usually in the form of the *vitz*, a philosophical witticism, or a *vitzl*, its diminutive, which was a little joke or pun.

For two generations Americans have heard this kind of humor, or its derivation, on radio and TV, in the movies and night clubs; Jewish comedians from Danny Kaye to Milton Berle, from Jack Leonard to Jack Benny have made America laugh by broadcasting the spirit that animated the ghetto. And I have heard Jewish intellectuals pun, wisecrack and joke for hours, sitting around a table in a coffeehouse.

The ghetto Jew never asked for sympathy; he was never a bore and he was never bored.

If he was out to succeed in business, he was not out to exclude everything else. He was, for example, almost always a reader. I remember the pushcart peddler who read books on the job: how rude he could be to a potential customer, as if to say—what nerve! intruding on my reading; Or the guy who sold scholarly books and had to question every customer before he would close a sale. Always he put two or three test questions to the customer and if he was not satisfied with the answers, he would shake his head, replace the book on the shelf and say, "Leave the book. It's not for you, believe me, sir." Very polite he was, but firm.

And the *schnorrers,* the professional beggars of the ghetto, how they elevated their "work" to a fine art! "If it was not for me," the *schnorrer* would tell his "mark," "how would you accumulate the necessary quota of *mitsves,* good deeds to be added upon the day of reckoning?" And then he would be overbearing and indignant about it too as he pocketed your dollar. The greatest case of a true *schnorrer,* the essence of *schnorrer*dom, involved me personally not many years ago. One of these ghetto gentlemen stopped by my home in Charlotte, North Carolina, explaining that he was on his way to Miami for the winter months. I picked up the phone and registered him in a downtown hotel. A single room—I said to the desk clerk, "With a shower and TV," said the *schnorrer,* who was standing at my elbow. The next morning the local rabbi gave the *schnorrer* breakfast; a downtown businessman gave him lunch; and the treasurer of the temple bought him a bus ticket.

On the Lower East Side our parents spoke to us in Yiddish and we answered in English. As a result, a proverb circulated around the ghetto: "In America the children bring up the parents." Most of the old folks struggled to learn the new language, then by and by gave up on it, having mastered at least enough words to give their Yiddish a strong flavor of American. Any one of their sentences might contain a sprinkling of terms such as *haircut, grocery, teacher, office, paycheck, wedding, doctor,* or *bill-collector.* The Yiddish accent with grotesque pronunciations became a feature of vaudeville humor in the 1920s and '30s. But soon the dialect jokes became an anachronism— they made little sense when the greenhorn's grandson was in medical school and the granddaughter was up at Radcliffe.

One of the earliest and continuing processes in ghetto life

was the hurry up to be assimilated. The kids insisted on speaking English to their parents and tried to get the old man to trim his beard in the style of Ulysses S. Grant, or to shave it off altogether. "Why don't you shave and get a haircut!" The cry of today's conservative oldster to the hairy hippie, was on the Lower East Side reversed. Clothing, too, played a big role in the process of Americanization, and anything suggesting the old country was naturally considered a bit embarrassing, at least to the youngsters. For some reason the older generation thought that a gold watch and chain, or a gold pin-watch with fleur-de-lis for the ladies, was the ultimate in American style. Peddlers who extended credit did a flourishing business in these two items, and in general at least some sort of a timepiece was considered essential to the greenhorn starting his new life in America. One of my cousins came to our house carrying a suitcase in one hand and an alarm clock in the other. Only thirty minutes off the boat and cleared through immigration officials, he had been pressured by a peddler to spend a dollar ninety-five on this first step in naturalization—a clock.

Frequently, it was the Tammany Hall worker who advised the immigrants about taking out first papers for citizenship and about night-school classes that taught English, current events and American history. If the newcomer was a *singleman* (unmarried), he was often introduced speedily to the *shadkhan* (marriage broker).

Soon the newcomers caught on to one of America's basic rhythms—the drive for status through money. The many solitary "readers" became peddlers, teachers or door-to-door salesmen; many became *shadkhanim*; some functioned as rabbis, except without any formal training or ordination. My father was one of these "readers" who took up free-lance journalism and got a license to perform civil marriages. In this way he managed to contribute five hundred dollars to the household during the course of an average year.

At the same time, the Jews had a high proportion of skilled workers among each new shipload of immigrants—higher in fact than any other ethnic group. The Jews were needle-trade workers, cobblers, milliners, furriers, etc. Many of them plainly and simply were tailors. At the beginning of this century it was the immigrant Jews who created the American ready-made clothing industry. In 1889 Americans spent four hundred and forty million dollars on ready-made clothing; twenty-five years later gross sales for this same commodity had advanced to one billion, three hundred million dollars.

Because many of the immigrants were Orthodox Jews who had to observe the Sabbath and many holy days during the year, and because they looked a bit "foreign" and spoke English poorly or not at all, there was a fear among the ghetto people of being unemployable on the American business market. These conditions led to an enormous drive to be self-employed or to work for other immigrant Jews. Many such arrangements were indeed made, and I remember factories and shops closing down on Friday afternoon and remaining shut all day Saturday. This during the era of the six-day working week.

Another expedient maneuver was to obtain employment as a contractor for an American firm and to remain unobtrusively in the background. A cousin of mine manufactured shirts in a small shop that employed three seamstresses. The fellow could speak perhaps less than a dozen words in English, but he filled orders from Macy's. His chances of working directly for Macy's, in person, were slim, and he knew it. So instead of showing up at Macy's employment office he sent a sample of his work to their purchasing office. In this way he was more or less "employed by Macy's" for many years.

But to understand the workaday situation on the Lower East Side you must imagine each tenement flat as a self-contained garment shop, with boss, overseer and employee busily pressing and sewing for twelve, sometimes fifteen hours a day. In one room you might find four men, one or two women, a few teen-age girls and perhaps one eleven-year-old boy, all working on knee pants, or "knickers" as they were called by workers and customers alike. They did piecework, averaging about seventy-five cents for a dozen pairs—which meant approximately fifteen dollars a week for a family of five. Labor laws were easily circumvented by giving all the young people the title of "learners" or "temporary employees." Hot irons were kept ready all through the heat of the summer, which was the busy season for knee-pants workers. Boarders sometimes worked along with the family occupying the flat; they paid two and a half dollars a week for a place to sleep and breakfast every morning. Everyone pitched in and worked long hours to reach the goal of twenty dozen pairs of knickers per week. During that time the eleven-year-old boy would earn just enough to buy himself one pair of knickers.

Five months out of the year the knee-pants business was off season, at which time the men would strap their sewing machines on their backs and go from factory to factory, looking for work.

A few blocks north of my own street in the Lower East Side was Stanton Street, where the experienced tailors worked with their families to make men's coats at an average rate of twenty-seven cents per coat. The garment was delivered to the contractor complete except for the buttons and buttonholes which the contractor would let out elsewhere.

In the years 1912–14 the industry became unionized, much to the sorrow of these simple tenement flat workers, who were afraid that because of unionization they would lose their one source of livelihood. In those days free enterprise had a true and basic meaning for the immigrant Jews, who learned, practiced and deeply believed in this fundamental economic principle of American life.

One veritable institution of ghetto life was the pushcart peddler, who sold various items from tin cups (two cents each), to eyeglasses (thirty-five cents the pair). The peddler who sold eyeglasses kept a mirror attached to a stick—this so the customer might "fit himself." Eyeglasses were a sign of status. They made a man appear a scholar, and many of the sidewalk photographers carried a supply of spectacles so that you might be posed as a very serious book-reading type of gentleman. (The snapshot would be sent to relatives in the old country or proudly placed on the mantelpiece over the fake fireplace in the parlor.)

There were peddlers who sold geese and chickens, hung by their necks from the pushcarts. There was a guy who sold horse radish, his churning machine padlocked to a lamppost. There were suspenders peddlers crying their wares up and down the streets; on rainy days, the suspenders man sold umbrellas.

Dr. Miriam Beard of Princeton makes an interesting point in her book *Jews in a Gentile World*. She says that business empires, like all other empires, crumble and decay. The rich businessmen grow lazy and lose initiative and alertness. No society, says Dr. Beard, has ever enjoyed commercial supremacy twice. Her strong implication is that the Jews have survived as an active, successful group throughout all periods of history because they have *never* enjoyed commercial supremacy in any of the countries in which they have lived. Small successes and out-of-the-mainstream achievement, certainly. The Jews have often managed this kind of commercial accomplishment; but outright supremacy, never. If Dr. Beard's thesis is valid, and I see no reason to doubt it, this has been fortunate for the Jews.

In any case, out of the working conditions of the Lower East Side emerged a succession of developments that were awesome, terrible and in their way inspiring—not merely for their influence on immigrant Jews, but for their impact on America at large. One of these was the rise of Socialism fostered and to some extent initiated by Abraham Cahan, editor of the *Jewish Daily Forward* and author of the classic novel of immigrant life in America, *The Rise of David Levinsky*.

The other developments were the formation of labor unions and the mass strikes which took place during the years 1900–14. This momentous period in American labor history is now known as the Great Revolt, and it was set in motion largely by the garment workers' situation in sweatshops and tenement flats on the Lower East Side of New York City.

The tragic fire in the Triangle Shirtwaist Factory in 1911, which claimed the lives of more than one hundred forty employees, was one of the turning points in the battle for decent working conditions. When needle-trades workers went on strike, from then on all New York became involved. Uptown Gentiles came to the assistance of the sweatshop workers. Christian clergymen and churchwomen from all over the city picketed with the shop girls.

When settlements were finally made the sweatshop was abolished forever, piecework in the factory and the home was outlawed. Workers were given higher pay, shorter days and decent working conditions. The influence of the new labor unions extended also into New York's political life and helped to elect officials to the state legislature and even to wield considerable weight in mayoralty and gubernatorial contests.

The role of the Jews in American political life has been vigorous and many-sided; no doubt the subject contains ample material for a lengthy book. But something of the scope and range of Jewish participation in this field may be very faintly suggested by statements from three leading members of the Christian establishment in the United States, covering half a century of activity in social reform. In 1912 William Howard Taft told reporters that "Jews make the best Republicans." Around the same time William Travers Jerome, district attorney of New York City, scolded an audience of metropolitan aristocrats for their lack of interest in social improvement. "The only civic and welfare work being done in this city," said Mr. Jerome, "is being done by the Irish Catholic charities and Russian Jews on the Lower East Side." In the early 1950s the late Adlai Stevenson told a confidant: "The Jews make the best Democrats."

The Jewish Labor Union has been a great influence upon the non-Jewish labor unionists. For example the first written contract between management and labor was called the "protocol of peace" in 1910, a signed agreement by Hart Schaffner & Marx that established an industrial court as a substitute for a constant strike. This protocol became a model for industrial peace for modern trade unionism. The International Ladies Garment Workers Union boasted just a few years ago that it had had no strike in the dress industry in the last twenty years. The Amalgamated Labor Unions were extending loans to employers in distress, and a few years ago David Dubinsky of the International Ladies Garment Workers made money available to the Rockefellers for a housing project in Puerto Rico.

What impresses itself immediately about the "Bintel Brief" letters is the remarkable language by some of the writers—much like the letters of English seamen in Shakespeare's day who wrote home in brilliant English and with beautiful phraseology.

Here are a few samples of these expressions I found in the "Bintel Brief":

I harnessed myself to the wagon of family life and pulled with all my strength.

This is the voice of one who is buried but not covered by earth, tied down but not in chains, silenced but not muted, whose heart is human but yet unlike other human beings.

A gloomy year has gone by since these sufferings hold me in thrall.

And a son leaving for America talks about his mother saying good-by to him:

There was no shaking of the alms box, you do that at funerals, there was no grave digging, but I myself put on the white shirt that was wet with my mother's tears and climbed into the wagon.

When our big mouth "workers' liberator" Theodore Roosevelt was elected for a second term, it got so bad I couldn't find a job.

I am an old woman of seventy, writing this letter with my heart's blood because I am worried.

My heart bounded with joy when I saw New York in the distance. It was like coming to the World City where everything breathed in freedom where I can become a proletarian.

. . . but the jingling of the silver brought me no solace, and the glitter of gold did not ease my pain.

The 'Jewish immigrants from Russia, Poland, Hungary were literally born again when they landed on the golden shore of America.

Yet there were congressmen and senators forever on the lookout to stop this immigration. In 1908 there was a law passed making it necessary for an immigrant to show twenty-five dollars in cash before he could land. But where could they get the twenty-five dollars? And many of them were sent back to Russia and Poland or Rumania. Another fear of the immigrant was trachoma and the separation of families, the mother with trachoma being held for deportation, allowing the children and the father to enter; or a child with trachoma being separated from its family and being sent back to Europe.

The McCarran-Walter Act of the 1950s sealed the border against those from Eastern Europe and the Mediterranean, and the "more desirable" immigrants from northern Europe were made welcome.

Basically America has offered the Jewish immigrant hope, the hope to enter the open society without hindrance. Mobility. I'll take that as a synonym for America any time. Because this mobility has no parallel anywhere in the world. America is a promise of the opportunity to enter the open society on your own merits; to go from one income level to another income level, to go from one place to another place without interference and to go from one economic and social class to another economic and social class.

America gave us immigrants a guarantee . . . a guarantee as secure as those written in constitutions and charters.

This guarantee was that if you studied hard and worked hard and read books you could enter the open society of America.

There was never a more even trade.

The immigrants repaid America a thousandfold. We were poor on the Lower East Side of New York, very poor, far poorer I suspect than the poor in America now, but we had a strategy for defeating poverty and many of us did defeat it. Those who did not may not have felt that life was fine and brilliant; indeed they may have felt life was hard and cruel, but they did not feel it was empty either.

The fact is that the greatest intellectual and economic developments have come to those lands who sent their sons to a neighbor and received the sons of the neighbor in return. Look at those nations which have not had this exchange and you will see the torpid mass.

In the United States as late as 1900, fewer than one third of our people could trace their ancestry further than a native-born grandfather. Essentially we are all foreigners. Indeed, based on European standards, all Americans, even today in 1970, are foreigners.

And how lucky for America that millions of these foreigners were Jews from Eastern Europe.

What some of our superpatriots call the "less desirable" immigrants. This was the luckiest thing that ever happened to the United States of America. Because if the truth were known, the "more desirable" immigrants from northern Europe looked down on the United States in the mid-nineteenth and early twentieth centuries. They shook their heads in sorrow and chagrin; ah, no Shakespeare, no Beethoven, no Goethe, no Schubert, just a bunch of frontiersmen killing Indians and looking to make money. Read the speeches of Charles Dickens made in England after a year in America, just a bunch of money grabbers, he said . . . will take another thousand years for them to produce a Shakespeare, a Milton, and presumably a Dickens. And from France, Pierre Loti; ah, you should read his essays after a visit here: frontiersmen, shoot 'em up, money grabbers, nothing. How could these "less desirable" immigrants feel without Goethe, Beethoven, Schubert, Rousseau, Joan of Arc, Shakespeare?

On the other hand what the superpatriots call the Jews, the "less desirable," were the original "ground kissers" of America. These were the immigrants who kissed the ground when they got off the gangplank because they saw hope, indeed were born again. Precisely because most of them had to learn a new language, this vitality was added to, because when you're learning a new language you are indeed born again. It was this gulf stream of vitality that helped make America. And not because these Eastern European and Mediterranean immigrants were better than the natives. Of course not. In fact this immigrant did not think himself as good as the native, and it was precisely this sense of inferiority that gave him his tremendous drive to make good, and in the process to help make America.

Before World War I many immigrants, particularly Italians, went back to Europe. At this time some of the superpatriots were agitating for a restrictive immigration clause and they carefully documented the names of these immigrants who went back to Europe, taking millions of dollars of savings back with them. President Wilson looked at that imposing list and said, "They left us the subways they built, didn't they?"

A famous railroad tycoon once said, "Give me Swedes, snuff and whiskey and I will build a railway to heaven."

But the bill restricting immigration passed, and if we think we got by with something cute we are sadly mistaken. In 1970, with over two hundred million people, there are less patents for new ideas registered than there were in 1912 when we had only one hundred million people. How many electrical wizards like Charles Steinmetz did we keep out of the United States since 1920? How many Joseph Goldbergers? The name Joseph Goldberger may not be familiar to you. He was a Hungarian Jew, a doctor, who went to live in Negro cabins of the Deep South and eventually discovered the cure for pellagra. How many millions of Southern children have grown up with straight legs because of this Jewish immigrant? We'll never know. And we'll never know how many Joseph Goldbergers were kept out of the United States, either. The dice of God are always loaded.

The one section of our country which is only now entering the industrial age is the old Confederate South; significantly, this is the one section that had none of these "less desirable" immigrants. Of course there was great comfort in the homogeneous society, each man seeing an image of himself in every other man. Yet consider this—because the South did not have any of this Eastern European immigration between 1870 and 1914, and because the South had also segregated one third of its population, the South's second biggest export next to cotton, during that seventy-year period, was its brains.

Perhaps that is America's good fortune, to have had the marginal man struggling to get "in," struggling to prove himself, struggling to enter the open society and struggling to become like everybody else as quickly as possible.

The American institutions provide us with this living symbol of what we are and what we ought to be. The fulfillment of the biblical injunction of Nehemiah to seek the peace of the city in which you live, to protect it from harm, and this awareness of the human story; the healing of the sick and afflicted, the easing of pain, the recognition of the sacredness of a single human being. It is this awareness of the sacredness of the individual which mankind owes to the Jews. The wonderful Greeks filled the world with intellectuality, created the academy, the drama and architecture; and the equally wonderful Romans, who created the structure of the city, our law, and engineering of the dams, aqueducts and roads throughout the world; but neither the Greeks nor the Romans really recognized the sacredness of the single human being. This came from the Hebrews.

The Greeks and the Romans put their aged and their blind outside the city gates; the Jews made them the guests of honor. When the aged and the blind came into your home on a Sabbath you got out of your chair and they sat down.

When the Jews fled to America from the persecutions of Russia and Poland they sought in this new land the basis of all civil rights: the rights to a home, work, family and citizenship, and to a large degree they succeeded in achieving these goals. It is these successes that the "Bintel Brief" reveals.

But above all in this collection there is The Human Story, indeed ten thousand human-interest stories in the letters and biographies published in these "Bintel Brief" letters. There are stories of broken homes, and husbands deserting their families. On the other hand, there are many stories of great nobility among these people.

There are many stories of mothers and daughters-in-law and of loneliness, and the girls who work to support their husbands in school. This was known as "holding the book" for a fellow. Presumably she holds the book to him while he's studying. The conflict that arose from this was that many a scholar became a doctor or a lawyer and then discarded his uneducated wife.

There is the story of the boy who quit chemistry lessons because he was told that a graduate chemist could not get a job if he was a Jew, and there are some stories of white slavery, immigrant girls lured to a house of prostitution and kept captive in it.

A wife is distressed because the husband visits the grave of his first wife, and another wife is distressed because her husband has a double headstone on the grave of his first wife and a place for himself.

There's a story of the Jewish immigrant who became an evangelist to the Jews and later repented of his treachery.

There are many disagreements in these letters over the keeping of *kosher*. The parents who keep a *kosher* home and the daughter-in-law who does not keep *kosher*.

The letters give an insight into the lives of the Jewish immigrants to America. And they were not wholly concerned with their private affairs, but with the politics and events surrounding them as well, including discussion of the women's suffrage, prohibition and World War I.

These are stories of socialists, anarchists, freethinkers, and the Orthodox. There is also evidence that we had a turn-of-the-century hippie movement among the immigrant Jews; their individualism and their cry for social justice were very much like that of the flower children of our 1960s. But throughout all it is the evidence that the human story really involves a man and a woman. No matter how high we go into outer space, no matter how many planets we eventually explore, the human story will remain the same as it was a thousand years ago, as it will be a thousand years hence, and it involves a man, and a woman and children, their joys and their sorrows, their pleasures and their tribulations.

Harry Golden

Mr. Golden's comments on the letters appear in italics.

A Bintel Brief

1906

Esteemed Editor,

I hope that you will advise me in my present difficulty.

I am a "greenhorn," only five weeks in the country, and a jeweler by trade. I come from Russia, where I left a blind father and a stepmother. Before I left, my father asked me not to forget him. I promised that I would send him the first money I earned in America.

When I arrived in New York I walked around for two weeks looking for a job, and the bosses told me it was after the season. In the third week I was lucky, and found a job at which I earn eight dollars a week. I worked, I paid my landlady board, I bought a few things to wear, and I have a few dollars in my pocket.

Now I want you to advise me what to do. Shall I send my father a few dollars for Passover, or should I keep the little money for myself? In this place the work will end soon and I may be left without a job. The question is how to deal with the situation. I will do as you tell me.

Your thankful reader,
I.M.

ANSWER:

The answer to this young man is that he should send his father the few dollars for Passover because, since he is young, he will find it easier to earn a living than would his blind father in Russia.

1906

Dear Editor,

I hope that you will give me the opportunity to tell the world about my sufferings.

Two years ago when I was barely nineteen I left my home in a small town in Russia. I had read many books that stimulated my imagination and I dreamed of becoming a countess, or at least a millionaire.

After father died, my mother received a letter from his brother in America saying that, since he heard times were bad for us, he wanted me to come to him. Later he would also bring my mother over. He wrote that he was wealthy, and with him I would live like a princess. My mother and I agreed that I should go to the rich uncle, and I left for America.

From the day I arrived, my uncle was exceptionally good to me. When I entered the world of luxury I felt that all of my dreams were coming true. His wealth and his indulgence excited me, and as I now recall, I didn't care that he was becoming more and more familiar in his attitude to me. I didn't even feel misgivings when my uncle became more intimate with me or when he seduced me. Any regrets I had were submerged in my infatuation. I became his constant mistress.

About eight or nine months ago a young couple came from New York to the town where my uncle lives. Since the man had a brother in town, a man with whom my uncle had business dealings, I became acquainted with the young couple. The man was handsome, polite, decent, and my uncle thought highly of him. The only thing against him was that he spoke like a Socialist.

One day when the young man was in our house, my uncle suggested that he become my tutor. He remarked that I was still "green" and knew very little English. The young man became my tutor, and I am not ashamed to say that I cherished the opportunity to spend time with him. The man interested me more than his English and his whole education. In time, however, his good manners and polite attitude awakened in me an interest in learning. He taught me not only English, but an understanding of life and man's struggle for justice. He helped me understand the meaning of Socialism.

His sweet wife, too, became my teacher and I learned a great deal from both of them. But hear how I repaid them for their kindness.

Suddenly I realized that I was pregnant. I told my uncle I was to become a mother, and to my astonishment he answered cold-bloodedly that something would be done about it. I didn't want to undergo such a criminal operation, and told him I would tell everyone the truth. He said, "Fool, who would believe you!" (He was a prominent man and a trustee in the synagogue.) Soon he came up with another suggestion: he would say I was seduced by my tutor.

Naturally, I could not agree to the vile proposal, to smear the good name of such a decent and innocent person. My uncle ignored me, however, and carried out his evil plan. He declared that the man was never to come to his house again, because I had said he had seduced me. I had neither the opportunity nor the courage to clear the innocent man, and I was tormented. Once the young man forced his way into my uncle's house. From my rooms I heard him shouting that I should confront him before everybody and say he was guilty. I started toward the room with the impulse to cry out that he was innocent, and I wanted to tell everybody of my uncle's wickedness. But I was overcome by emotion and fell to the floor in a faint.

The same day I was taken to the hospital in a critical condition. And thus, because of me, was a decent good man's reputation sullied. When I left the hospital, I did not return to my "rich uncle." I live alone now, lonely and poor. My aim in life is to announce to the world who was guilty in my misfortune and to clear the name of my good teacher. Maybe I'll have the chance to fall at his feet and beg him for forgiveness. I beg you to publish my letter in the name of the innocent man.

Sincerely,
H.P.

ANSWER:

We print this letter primarily in the interests of the innocent young man. If the letter writer's uncle is really as she pictures him, he is one of the most degenerate creatures on earth. Nevertheless, the writer of the letter should never have allowed this false accusation to be made against the young man.

1906

Dear Editor,

Since I have been a *Forward* reader from the early days, I hope you will allow me to unburden my heart in the "Bintel Brief."

Nineteen years ago, when I was a child, I came to America. Later I was married here. I was never rich financially, but wealthy in love. I loved my husband more than anything in the world. We had seven children, the oldest is now thirteen. But God did not want us to be happy, and after years of hard work, my husband developed consumption.

When does a working man go to Colorado? When he has one foot in the grave.

When I began to talk to my husband about his going to Colorado, he answered that he couldn't leave me alone with the children, and he kept working till he collapsed. When I was pregnant with my seventh child, I finally sent him away.

As time went on, he wrote me that he was feeling better, and no one was as happy as I. I counted the minutes till I could be with my husband again. Meanwhile, I had a baby and had to make the *bris* alone. When my baby was three months old, I took my seven children and went to my husband.

My husband told me he had opened a small business in Colorado, and hoped to make a living. But I heard him cough, and when I questioned him, he answered with a bitter smile that there was no cure for this illness. I immediately saw my tragedy and wouldn't let him work. I went out peddling with a basket, and left him at home with the children. I tried to make a living, I got a little aid, but my husband became gradually weaker.

For about fourteen months my husband didn't leave his bed. I was willing to do the hardest work to keep him alive. I fought my bitter lot like a lion, to chase the angel of death from my husband, but alas, he won. I was left alone and poor, with seven little orphans. With my husband's death my spirit and courage died, and I neglected my house and children.

My friends were afraid I might go mad, and they convinced me to go back to New York. I arrived at ten o'clock of a rainy November night and stood in the street with my children, broken and tired, with no place to go, my tears mingling with the falling rain.

Imagine how I felt then—I set out with the children to seek my husband's sister. I cannot describe the scene when I came to her that night and told her of the death of her only brother. I had decided that if she would not take me in, I would throw myself into the river.

But I found comfort with his poor sister. She kept me and the children four weeks, and during this time I placed four of the children in an orphanage. I am now left with three, but I cannot earn a living. If I were to go back to Colorado with the three children, I could make a living peddling, and could possibly plan a future for the four when they got out of the orphanage. There they would have the fresh air, here I am afraid they might inherit their father's sickness. But it is hard for me to leave the four. I am brokenhearted every time I go to see them. I live here in dreary infested rooms, I can't earn a living, and my heart draws me there, where my husband died. Of what use is the great city with its people when for me it is narrow and dark?

With tear-filled eyes I beg you, dear Editor, to advise me what to do. Maybe through you I will find solace for my broken heart.

Your constant reader,
A Young Widow

ANSWER:
We believe the writer's duty demands that she go to Colorado to work there with the hope that in a short time she will be able to have her four children from the orphanage with her. Her devotion to her children will help her overcome her troubles and give her consolation.

1906

Worthy Editor,

We are a small family who recently came to the "Golden Land." My husband, my boy and I are together, and our daughter lives in another city.

I had opened a grocery store here, but soon lost all my money. In Europe we were in business; we had people working for us and paid them well. In short, there we made a good living but here we are badly off.

My husband became a peddler. The "pleasure" of knocking on doors and ringing bells cannot be known by anyone but a peddler. If anybody does buy anything "on time," a lot of the money is lost, because there are some people who never intend to pay. In addition, my husband has trouble because he has a beard, and because of the beard he gets beaten up by the hoodlums.

Also we have problems with our boy, who throws money around. He works every day till late at night in a grocery for three dollars a week. I watch over him and give him the best because

I'm sorry that he has to work so hard. But he costs me plenty and he borrows money from everybody. He has many friends and owes them all money. I get more and more worried as he takes here and borrows there. All my talking doesn't help. I am afraid to chase him away from home because he might get worse among strangers. I want to point out that he is well versed in Russian and Hebrew and he is not a child any more, but his behavior is not that of an intelligent adult.

I don't know what to do. My husband argues that he doesn't want to continue peddling. He doesn't want to shave off his beard, and it's not fitting for such a man to do so. The boy wants to go to his sister, but that's a twenty-five-dollar fare. What can I do? I beg you for a suggestion.

Your constant reader,
F.L.

ANSWER:
Since her husband doesn't earn a living anyway, it would be advisable for all three of them to move to the city where the daughter is living. As for the beard, we feel that if the man is religious and the beard is dear to him because the Jewish law does not allow him to shave it off, it's up to him to decide. But if he is not religious, and the beard interferes with his earnings, it should be sacrificed.

1906

Dear Editor,

For a long time I worked in a shop with a Gentile girl, and we began to go out together and fell in love. We agreed that I would remain a Jew and she a Christian. But after we had been married for a year, I realized that it would not work.

I began to notice that whenever one of my Jewish friends comes to the house, she is displeased. Worse yet, when she sees me reading a Jewish newspaper her face changes color. She says nothing, but I can see that she has changed. I feel that she is very unhappy with me, though I know she loves me. She will soon become a mother, and she is more dependent on me than ever.

She used to be quite liberal, but lately she is being drawn back to the Christian religion. She gets up early Sunday mornings, runs to church and comes home with eyes swollen from crying. When we pass a church now and then, she trembles.

Dear Editor, advise me what to do now. I could never convert, and there's no hope for me to keep her from going to church. What can we do now?

Thankfully,
A Reader

ANSWER:

Unfortunately, we often hear of such tragedies, which stem from marriages between people of different worlds. It's possible that if this couple were to move to a Jewish neighborhood, the young man might have more influence on his wife.

Mixed marriage between Gentile and Jew is a complicated affair.

According to the latest statistics, it occurs eight times oftener with a Jewish male and a Gentile female than with a Jewish female and a Gentile male. But it is complicated because it can seldom be an ordinary boy-meets-girl proposition. The Jew must almost always bring something else to the union besides himself. The girl must justify her marriage to a Jew: "I married a Jew, but he's a composer, a writer, a journalist, a physicist, a college professor," or "I married a Jew but he's rich." A Gentile girl will rarely marry a Jewish shipping clerk or the Jew who pumps gas at a filling station. She almost always enters a higher economic level than that from which she came.

Much has been written and said about the terrible scene that takes place in a Jewish home when a son marries a shikse—the parents sit shiva in mourning for the boy. But not enough has been said about the Gentile family. For while the parents of the Gentile girl may accept the Jewish son-in-law and tolerate the marriage, the girl loses many of her friends, former classmates and relatives.

The mixed marriage can be most successful among those who are self-sustaining by career, notably entertainers, actors, artists, sculptors and writers.

But the attempt to reflect the melting-pot culture of the society in which we live has continued to lead to increased intermarriage.

And there are many letters in the "Bintel Brief" concerning this phenomenon, and the sorrow of parents over the prospect of their son marrying a Gentile. The answer which the editor of the Forward gave to these letters was sensible. In effect he said that marriage under the best of circumstances, in which the partners to the union come from the same background, the same religion, the same economic status, presents a great problem for success. And when you add the obstacle of intermarriage to the existing problems it could, he said, lead to disaster.

1906

Honorable Editor,

I have a grievous wound in my heart and maybe through the "Bintel Brief" I will find relief.

I am a young woman. I was happily married, but a year ago death suddenly took my husband. He was handsome and I am considered attractive. When we used to walk together we often heard the comment, "What a good-looking couple." We were in love and faithful to each other in the full sense of the word.

When he died and left me with our only daughter, fifteen years of age, my world collapsed. I was in despair but not for financial reasons. My husband left a generous policy, quite a bit of money, and I run a successful business.

I cried till my eyes were swollen, and when they laid my dear husband in the coffin and took it out of the house, I fainted four times. In the carriage on the way to the cemetery I sat in a daze. My daughter and a young man, my husband's best friend, were with me.

When they covered my husband's coffin I became hysterical, screamed and tried to stop them. Finally they dragged me away from the grave and calmed me down.

My husband's friend didn't leave my side. They had been comrades since they came to America, prepared to face any dangers for each other. The friend had been like a member of the family in our house and my daughter was very attached to him. The friend was not as handsome, well built or attractive as my husband and he had never shown the least interest in me as a woman. Nor had I ever thought of him as anything but a friend. Suddenly this changed.

I don't know how it happened that during the drive home from the cemetery I was alone in the carriage with my husband's friend. He told me later that it was pure chance. Seated in the carriage, I began to cry again, and the friend comforted me, patted my hands and begged me not to endanger my health. As if in a dream, a thought came to me: Isn't this more than friendly sympathy, isn't this perhaps the interest of a man in a woman? In my sorrow and confusion I didn't know what was happening to me. As he comforted me, the friend began to kiss my hands and I looked at him in amazement. Instead of drawing back, though, he began to stroke my hair and swore that he felt toward his dead friend's wife as toward an unhappy sister. He spoke with tears in his eyes, drew me to him and kissed me passionately. Those were passionate kisses from a man to a woman, but they were mingled with his tears for the death of his dear friend and for my fate.

I had no will to protest and he held me and kissed me again

and again. And then I heard words of love from him. I felt like a sinner. When I got home I was afraid to look my daughter in the eyes. I imagined I heard my husband calling me a hypocrite and saying my tears were false.

The next morning my husband's friend came to my house. He cried bitterly and told me he felt like a traitor, but he loved me so much that he would waste away if I didn't become his. He begged me in his friend's name to marry him and then he could show his faithfulness to his friend's family.

Dear Editor, I swear to you that in my heart there was only one love, for my husband, but I am a weak woman and I couldn't fight against the passionate pleas and kisses. I was helpless and I gave him my word when my husband was barely two weeks in the grave. I told him I would marry him a year after my husband's death. But I feel guilty toward my husband. My daughter realized everything. With tears in her eyes, she blurted out that her father's grave was not an hour old when I already had taken a new bridegroom. Her words hurt me, and I had no answer. But in time she accepted him.

My close friends advise me to marry my husband's friend, and I will do so because I know that he will be good to my daughter and to me. But before the wedding I would like your opinion on all that has happened to me.

Sincerely,
B.V.

ANSWER:

The woman's excuse that she was unable to protest against the passionate advances of her husband's friend is a weak one. Better if she had opened the carriage door and asked him to get out. There is no excuse for the disgusting behavior of the young man. He should not have acted so shamefully after his friend's death. It is possible the widow is making a mistake in deciding to marry him, because it is doubtful whether she can be happy with such a man.

1906

Dear Editor,

Have pity on a suffering woman and advise me in the "Bintel Brief." I am in my twenties and have been in the country four years. I came here, a single girl, and, as is usual, I worked. After a while boys began to court me, but none of them appealed to me. One of them, a handsome boy from a fine family and a good wage earner, threw himself at my feet and begged me to marry him, but I didn't love him and chased him away. Thus time passed. Last year I met a young man, a few years older than I, a businessman with a good income. He soon fell in love with me. He began to bring me presents and begged me to say yes.

With this young man it was different than with the other boys. I didn't love them and I told them at once to leave me alone. For this young man I felt no love but I couldn't tell him. Each time he would come I wanted to return his gifts and tell him I wouldn't see him again, but when he came I couldn't open my mouth. Don't think he was so handsome or that he enchanted me. But he had some inner strength that affected me. He was one of those men who do not retreat till they've accomplished what they want.

Once he declared his love, my heart told me I would have trouble with him. I had no one here to advise me, and at one time I wanted to leave New York and so escape from him. But I stayed and did nothing. As time went on, he began to introduce me to his friends as his fiancée. Then he began to talk of renting an apartment. I want to say here that we are both freethinkers, but I didn't want to hear of just living together. He won out, however. He rented an apartment, furnished it, and ordered me to move my luggage and possessions there.

Dear Editor, it's possible I should be scolded for my actions, but believe me, I can't explain to myself why I obeyed him.

Well, we're living together now for the eighth month and I feel as if I'm losing my mind. I can't stand his bass voice—it's as if a saw were rasping my bones. I hate him, because he's a terrible egotist. When he starts talking about eating or sits at the table with the cigar in his mouth or pokes a toothpick around his teeth after eating I get so disgusted, I feel I am losing my senses.

He has a poor sister whose husband is a workingman, making a bare living. When he goes to his sister's they entertain him, but when she needs a few dollars for rent, he won't give her a cent. He tells her her husband is lazy, because anyone who doesn't make money is, in his eyes, an idler.

I have no tears left from crying. I want to save myself but cannot. I can't stand his talk, but when he is near me I lose control and become his slave. When he leaves I feel disgust and hatred. I want to escape from him because if I stay any longer I'll surely take my own life. Save me and advise me what to do.

Thankfully,
Unhappy

ANSWER:

The writer of this letter, we believe, could easily save herself. She could free herself if she really wanted to, if she had a strong enough character to accomplish it. From what she writes of her feelings toward the man, and from the story she relates, the best move would be for her to free herself.

1906

Dear Friend Editor,

Since your worthy newspaper has made it a policy in the "Bintel Brief" to allow everyone to state his opinions, ask questions and request advice, I hope you will allow me, too, to convey some part of my tragic life.

Thirteen years ago I loved and married a quiet young girl, and even in bad times we lived in peace and serenity. I worked hard. My wife devoted herself to our three children and the housekeeping.

A few years ago a brother of mine came to America too, with a friend of his. I worked in a shop, and as I was no millionaire, my brother and his friend became our boarders. Then my trouble began. The friend began earning good money. He began to mix in the household affairs and to buy things for my wife.

Neighbors began to whisper that my wife was carrying on an affair with this boarder, but I had no suspicions of my wife, whom I loved as life itself. I didn't believe them. Nevertheless I told her that people were talking. She swore to me that it was a lie, and evil people were trying to make bad blood between us. She cried as she spoke to me, and I believed her.

But people did not stop talking, and as time went on I saw that my wife was a common liar and that it was all true. My brother took it badly, because he had brought trouble into my home, and in remorse and shame, shot himself. He wounded himself and is left paralyzed on one side of his body. It was a terrible scandal. Good friends mixed in, made peace between us, and for the children's sake we remained together. I promised never to mention the tragic story and she promised to be a loyal wife to me and a good mother to the children she still loves deeply.

Again I worked long and hard, and with the aid of money I borrowed from friends I opened a stationery store. But my wife couldn't restrain herself and betrayed me again. She didn't give up her lover, but ran around with him day and night. I was helpless, because I had to be in the store at all times so she did as she pleased.

Again there was a scandal and her lover fled to Chicago. This was of little avail, because when my wife went to the country for the summer she left the children with the woman who rented her the rooms, and went to him for two weeks.

In short, I sold the store and everything is ruined. I gave her a thousand dollars and all her household effects. She and the children are now with him.

I know, dear Editor, that you cannot advise me now, but for me it's enough that I can pour out my suffering on paper. I can't find a place for myself. I miss the children. Life is dark and bitter without them. I hope that my wife will read my letter in the *Forward* and that she will blush with shame.

> With respect, your reader who longs
> for his wife and dear children,
> B.R.

1906

Worthy Editor,

I am a workingman from Bialystok, and there I belonged to the Bund. But I had to leave Bialystok, and later came to Minsk where I worked and joined the Socialist-Revolutionaries. What convinced me to join this organization is this: in Minsk there was a Bundist demonstration that was attacked by the police. They beat up the demonstrators brutally, and arrested many of them. The prisoners were lashed so severely that many of them became ill. One worker from Dvinsk was sentenced to fifty lashes, which caused him to develop epilepsy and while working in a factory he would suddenly fall in a fit.

When we, his co-workers, saw this, it aroused in us a desire for revenge against Czar Nicholas and his tyrannical police force. But when there was a convention of the Bund at that time, and they declared a policy against revenge, many of our Bund members joined the Socialist-Revolutionaries. I wanted to enter the militant organization, but war was declared against Japan, and since I was a reservist, I began to get mail from home advising me to flee to America. I let myself be talked into it and left.

I have been in the country now two years, and life is not bad. I work in a jewelry store, for good wages. But my heart will not remain silent within me over the blood of my brothers being spilled in Russia. I am restless because of the pogroms that took place in Bialystok, where I left old parents and a sister with three small children. I haven't heard from them since the pogrom and don't know if they're alive. But since they lived in the vicinity of the "Piaskes" where the Jewish defense group was located, it's possible they are alive.

Now I ask your advice. I cannot make up my mind whether to fulfill my duty to my parents and sister and bring them to America, if I hear from them, or to go back to Russia and help my brothers in their struggle.

If I had known what was going to happen there, I would not have gone to America. I myself had agitated that one should not leave for America but stay and fight in Russia till we were victorious. Now I feel like a liar and a coward. I agitated my friends, placed them in the danger of soldiers' guns and bullets. And I myself ran away.

Respectfully,
M.G.

ANSWER:

If one were to ask us the question before leaving Russia, we would not advise him to leave the revolutionary battlefields. Since the writer of the letter is already here and speaks of his two duties, we would like to tell him that the Assistance Movement in America is developing so rapidly that everyone who wants to be useful will be able to do enough here. He should bring his parents and sister here, and become active in the local movement.

The "Black Hundreds" organized by the League of Russian People threatened the Jews in Russia with bloody revenge for their participation in elections if they resulted in liberalizing the state.

The Black Hundreds was formed after 1881 with the introduc-

*tion of the "May laws." The laws set limitations on the employ-
ment of Christian domestics by Jews. It also limited the early
marriages of Jews, the use of Yiddish and Hebrew, and restricted
the Jews' entry into the universities.*

*Hand in hand with such restrictions went the limiting of
education for Jews in general, by placing quotas on their admission to high schools.*

*Military service in the Czar's army was compulsory. After
service, during which they had generally left their families in
great misery, many Jewish soldiers of the Czar returned, broken
in body and spirit. Jews therefore sought to evade the service in
every possible way and many of them found their voyage to
America their escape.*

1906

Dear Editor,

I am a Russian revolutionist and a freethinker. Here in
America I became acquainted with a girl who is also a freethinker.
We decided to marry, but the problem is that she has Orthodox
parents, and for their sake we must have a religious ceremony.
If we refuse the ceremony we will be cut off from them forever.
Her parents also want me to go to the synagogue with them
before the wedding, and I don't know what to do. Therefore I
ask you to advise me how to act.

Respectfully,
J.B.

ANSWER:
The advice is that there are times when it pays to give in to
old parents and not grieve them. It depends on the circumstances. When one can get along with kindness it is better not
to break off relations with the parents.

1906

Dear Editor,

I, too, want to take advantage of this opportunity to tell about my troubles, and I ask you to answer me.

Eight months ago I brought my girlfriend from Russia to the States. We had been in love for seven years and were married shortly after her arrival. We were very happy together until my wife became ill. She was pregnant and the doctors said her condition was poor. She was taken to the hospital, but after a few days was sent home. At home, she became worse, and there was no one to tend her.

You can hardly imagine our bitter lot. I had to work all day in the shop and my sick wife lay alone at home. Once as I opened the door when I came home at dinnertime, I heard my wife singing with a changed, hoarse voice. I was terror-stricken, and when I ran to her I saw she was out of her head with fever.

Imagine how I felt. My wife was so ill and I was supposed to run back to the shop because the last whistle was about to blow. Everybody was rushing back to work, but I couldn't leave. I knew that my boss would fire me. He had warned me the day before that if I came late again he wouldn't let me in. But how could I think of work now, when my wife was so ill? Yet without the job what would happen? There would not be a penny coming into the house. I stayed at my wife's bedside and didn't move till four o'clock.

Suddenly I jumped up and began to run around the room, in despair. My wife's singing and talking drove me insane. Like a madman I ran to the door and locked it. I leaped to the gas jet, opened the valve, then lay down in the bed near my wife and embraced her. In a few minutes I was nearer death than she.

Suddenly my wife cried out, "Water! water!" I dragged myself from the bed. With my last ounce of strength I crept to the door and opened it, closed the gas valve, and when I came to, gave her milk instead of water. She finished a glassful and wanted more, but there wasn't any more so I brought her some seltzer. I revived myself with water, and both of us slowly recovered.

The next morning they took my wife to the hospital, and after a stay of fourteen days she got well. Now I am happy that we are alive, but I keep thinking of what almost happened to us. Until now I never told anyone about it, but it bothers me. I have no secrets from my wife, and I want to know whether I should now tell her all, or not mention it. I beg you to answer me.

The Newborn

ANSWER:
This letter depicting the sad life of the worker is more powerful than any protest against the inequality between rich and poor. The advice to the writer is that he should not tell his wife that he almost ended both their lives. This secret may be withheld from his beloved wife, since it is clear he keeps it from her out of love.

1906

Dear Editor,

I am a young man of twenty-one; I have a seventeen-year-old cousin, and she and her parents would like me to marry her. I like the girl. She's educated, American-born, not bad-looking. But she's quite small.

That is the drawback: for her age, she is very short. And I happen to be tall. So when we walk down the street together, people look at us as a poorly matched couple. Another thing: she is very religious, and I am a freethinker. I ask you, esteemed Editor, could this lead to an unpleasant life if we were to marry? I wait impatiently for your answer.

Sympathetic

ANSWER:

Love conquers all. Many such couples live happily, and it is better for the man to be taller and the woman shorter, not the opposite. People are accustomed to seeing the man more developed than the woman. People stare? Let them stare! Also, the fact that the girl is religious and the man is not can be overcome if he has enough influence on her.

1906

Worthy Mr. Editor,

I was married six years ago in Russia. My husband had not yet been called up for the military service, and I married him because he was an only son and I knew he would not be taken as a soldier. But that year all originally exempted men were taken in our village. He had no desire to serve Czar Nickolai and since I didn't want that either, I sold everything I could and sent him to London. From there he went to America.

At first he wrote to me that it was hard for him to find work, so he couldn't send me anything to live on. I suffered terribly. I couldn't go to work because I was pregnant. And the harder my struggles became, the sadder were the letters from my husband. I suffered from hunger and cold, but what could I do when he was worse off than I?

Then his letters became fewer. Weeks and months passed without a word.

In time I went to the rabbi of our town and begged him to have pity on a deserted wife. I asked him to write to a

New York rabbi to find out what had happened to my husband. All kinds of thoughts ran through my mind, because in a big city like New York anything can happen. I imagined perhaps he was sick, maybe even dead.

A month later an answer came to the rabbi. They had found out where my husband was but didn't want to talk with him until I could come to America.

My relatives from several towns collected enough money for my passage and I came to New York, to the rabbi. They tricked my husband into coming there too. Till the day I die I'll never forget the expression on my husband's face when he unexpectedly saw me and the baby.

I was speechless. The rabbi questioned him for me, sternly, like a judge, and asked him where he worked and how much he earned. My husband answered that he was a carpenter and made twelve dollars a week.

"Do you have a wife, or are you single?" the rabbi asked. My husband trembled as he answered, "I have committed a crime," and he began to wipe his eyes with a handkerchief. And soon a detective appeared in the rabbi's house and arrested my husband, and the next day the story appeared in the Jewish newspapers. Then some good women who had pity on me helped me. They found a job for me, took me to lectures and theaters. I began to read books I had never realized existed.

In time I adjusted to life here. I am not lonely, and life for me and my child is quite good. I want to add here, too, that my husband's wife came to me, fell at my feet and cried, but my own problems are enough for me.

But in time my conscience began to bother me. I began to think of my husband, suffering behind bars in his dark cell. In dreams I see his present wife, who certainly loves him, and her little boy living in dire need without their breadwinner. I now feel differently about the whole thing and I have sympathy for my husband. I am even prepared, when he gets out of jail, to wish him luck with his new life partner, but he will probably be embittered toward me. I have terrible pangs of conscience and I don't know what I can do. I hope you will print my letter, and answer me.

Cordially,
Z.B.

ANSWER:
In the answer to this letter, the woman is comforted and praised for her decency, her sympathy for her husband and his second wife. Also it is noted that when the husband is released he will surely have no complaints against her, since he is the guilty one in the circumstances, not she.

1906

Dear Editor,

I am a girl from Galicia and in the shop where I work I sit near a Russian Jew with whom I was always on good terms. Why should one worker resent another?

But once, in a short debate, he stated that all Galicians were no good. When I asked him to repeat it, he answered that he wouldn't retract a word, and that he wished all Galician Jews dead.

I was naturally not silent in the face of such a nasty expression. He maintained that only Russian Jews are fine and intelligent. According to him, the *Galitzianer* are inhuman savages, and he had the right to speak of them so badly.

Dear Editor, does he really have a right to say this? Have the Galician Jews not sent enough money for the unfortunate sufferers of the pogroms in Russia? When a Gentile speaks badly of Jews, it's immediately printed in the newspapers and discussed hotly everywhere. But that a Jew should express himself so about his own brothers is nothing? Does he have a right? Are

Galicians really so bad? And does he, the Russian, remain fine and intelligent in spite of such expressions?

As a reader of your worthy newspaper, I hope you will print my letter and give your opinion.

With thanks in advance,
B.M.

ANSWER:

The Galician Jews are just as good and bad as people from other lands. If the Galicians must be ashamed of the foolish and evil ones among them, then the Russians, too, must hide their heads in shame because among them there is such an idiot as the acquaintance of our letter writer.

1906

Dear Editor,

In the name of all the workers of our shop, I write these words to you:

We work in a Bleecker Street shop, where we make raincoats. With us is a thirteen-year-old boy who works hard for the two and a half dollars a week he earns.

Just lately it happened that the boy came to work ten minutes late. This was a "crime" the bosses couldn't overlook, and for the lost ten minutes they docked him two cents. Isn't that a bitter joke?

Sincerely,
V.

1906

Dear Editor,

I join all the others who marvel at your "Bintel Brief," where almost everyone who has something on his conscience, or a secret, can express himself. I, too, wish to get something off my chest, and I want your advice.

I came to America as a *shokhet*. The ship I was on sank. I was among the lucky ones who were rescued, but my valise with my possessions, including the papers that certified that I am a *shokhet*, was lost.

Since I could no longer be a *shokhet*, I became a shirt-maker. Later I worked my way up and became a cloakmaker. But I was not satisfied because the physical labor and the degradation we had to endure in the shops was unbearable.

Within a few years two of my brothers came from Europe. We stayed together and we all worked in a shirt shop. Several times we tried contracting, but it didn't work out. At that time, white collars for shirts came into fashion. We had to sew on neckbands, to which the white collars were buttoned. This became a nuisance that delayed the work. Imagine having to cut out a band to fit each shirt we made. This wasn't easy, and the boss gave us the job of making the bands at home, as night work.

In short, one of us got an idea. Since the whole trade found the neckbands a problem, why not make the neckbands for all the manufacturers? Said and done! It worked out well. They snatched the bands from our hands and we were very busy. We were the only ones in the line from the start, and we prospered. Later a few more shops opened, but that didn't bother us because the trade grew even bigger.

Now we have a huge factory with our names on a big

sign on the front of the building. But the bands that gave us our start are no longer made by us alone. We have many workers but have paid little attention to them since we were so involved with making our fortune.

In time I began to read your newspaper and, out of curiosity, even the "Bintel Brief," to see what was going on in the world. As I read more and more about the troubles, my conscience awoke and I began to think: "Robber, cold-blooded robber." My conscience spoke to me: "Just look at your workers, see how pale and thin and beaten they look, and see how healthy and ruddy your face and hands are."

This conscience of mine has a strong voice. It yells at me just as I yell at my workers, and scolds me for all my offenses against them. It will be enough for me to give just a few samples of my evil deeds: The clock in our shop gets "fixed" twice a day; the hands are moved back and forth. The foreman has on his table a stick like a conductor's baton and when someone says a word during working hours he hears the tick-tock of that stick. Our wages are never under two dollars or over seven dollars a week.

My conscience bothers me and I would like to correct my mistakes, so that I will not have to be ashamed of myself in the future. But do not forget that my brothers do not feel as I do, and if I were to speak to them about all this they would consider me crazy. So what is left for me to do? I beg you, worthy Editor, give me a suggestion.

Yours sincerely,
B.

ANSWER:

We are proud and happy that through the *Forward* and the "Bintel Brief" the conscience of this letter writer was aroused. We can only say to the writer that he must not muffle the voice of his conscience. He will lose nothing, but will gain more and more true happiness.

1907

Dear Mr. Editor,

I have been in the country only two months, and I find myself in such terrible circumstances that I need your advice.

My father died when I was still a child. My mother was married a second time to a man who had a son from his first marriage. When the son went away to America my mother and stepfather decided I should marry him but didn't find it necessary to tell me about it.

Mother wrote to my stepbrother about the decision, and since he liked the idea, he sent me a steamship ticket. Still nothing was said to me about marriage. My mother told me only that my stepbrother was a good man, and that when I started earning money I was to pay him back for the steamship ticket. Things weren't good for me at home, and as everyone believed that in America money flowed in the streets, I decided to go.

Before I left, Mother told me that when my stepbrother came to take me from the ship I should say he was my bridegroom, otherwise they would not let me into the country.

At the age of seventeen I left my home, and when my stepbrother met me on my arrival in Castle Garden, I repeated what I had been told to say. Then they asked me and my stepbrother to hold up two fingers, a man said something, they told us to kiss each other, and they let me out.

I went off with my stepbrother, he bought me a few things, and he took me to a room where he had his own belongings. I looked around in wonder and asked him, "Are you going to live here with me?" Then he answered that I was no longer a stranger to him but his wife. I thought he was joking, but soon realized that he was serious and began to protest with all my might.

Two months have passed, and there hasn't been a day that we haven't had bitter fights. He shouts that he married me legally at Castle Garden. He's willing to go to the rabbi with me too, and threatens that he can have me arrested. I scream that he is not my husband and that I will pay him for the steamship ticket. I am working, I earn four dollars a week already, and I am willing to pay him a dollar a week, but he doesn't listen.

What's to be done? Give me some advice. It's impossible to live in the same room with him, because I have no more strength left to fight him off. I am almost out of my mind with worry. I beg you to answer immediately.

I thank you in advance,
Unhappy

ANSWER:
The advice to the writer of this letter is that she should go, with one of her friends who speaks English, to the police to lodge a complaint against the man who wants to force her to live with him. And if he persists in his claim that she is his legal wife, she must find a lawyer who will help her to have the marriage annulled.

1907

Worthy Editor,

I am eighteen years old and a machinist by trade. During the past year I suffered a great deal, just because I am a Jew.

It is common knowledge that my trade is run mainly by the Gentiles and, working among the Gentiles, I have seen things that cast a dark shadow on the American labor scene. Just listen:

I worked in a shop in a small town in New Jersey, with twenty Gentiles. There was one other Jew besides me, and both of us endured the greatest hardships. That we were insulted goes without saying. At times we were even beaten up. We work in an area where there are many factories, and once, when we were leaving the shop, a group of workers fell on us like hoodlums and beat us. To top it off, we and one of our attackers were arrested. The hoodlum was let out on bail, but we, beaten and bleeding, had to stay in jail. At the trial, they fined the hoodlum eight dollars and let him go free.

After that I went to work on a job in Brooklyn. As soon as they found out that I was a Jew they began to torment me so that I had to leave the place. I have already worked at many places, and I either have to leave, voluntarily, or they fire me because I am a Jew.

Till now, I was alone and didn't care. At this trade you can make good wages, and I had enough. But now I've brought my parents over, and of course I have to support them.

Lately I've been working on one job for three months and I would be satisfied, but the worm of anti-Semitism is beginning to eat at my bones again. I go to work in the morning as to Gehenna, and I run away at night as from a fire. It's impossible to talk to them because they are common boors, so-called "American sports." I have already tried in various ways, but the only way to deal with them is with a strong fist. But I am too weak and they are too many.

Perhaps you can help me in this matter. I know it is not an easy problem.

Your reader,
E.H.

ANSWER:

In the answer, the Jewish machinist is advised to appeal to the United Hebrew Trades and ask them to intercede for him and bring up charges before the Machinists Union about this persecution. His attention is also drawn to the fact that there are Gentile factories where Jews and Gentiles work together and get along well with each other.

Finally it is noted that people will have to work long and hard before this senseless racial hatred can be completely uprooted.

I remember a great factory, manufacturers of printing machinery, whose Gentile workers attacked a Jewish funeral procession

coming across the Williamsburg Bridge. They threw nuts and
bolts and pieces of iron at the mourners and many of them were
lying on the ground, holding their heads screaming in pain.
    An investigation was held but nothing came of it.

1907

Worthy Editor,

In the "Bintel Brief" I have already read about many kinds of problems, but never about such a misfortune as the one that befell me. I beg you to print my letter as quickly as possible and advise me how to save myself.

About four years ago, when I was still at home in Russia, a young man from another city boarded with us. When I decided to go to America he told me he wanted to go too. At the time I was nineteen years old. But my mother, who was a widow, said it was not proper for a girl and boy to make such a long journey together. She hinted that if we were planning to get married it would be all right. As long as I liked the young man, who was quiet and decent, I answered my mother that if he agreed I would too.

My mother began to talk to him, and he said it was impossible because he had a girl friend whom he was going to marry. Meanwhile, I fell in love with the young man. My love for him grew from day to day, until I couldn't restrain myself any longer, and I spoke to him openly about it. He listened to me attentively, and told me, too, that he was obligated to his sweetheart. When I asked him who she was and where she lived, he didn't answer me, but burst into tears. I was suffering, and decided to leave for America as soon as possible, in order to forget him.

When I finally got a steamship ticket from my aunt and began to get ready for the trip, the young man came to me one day and told me he loved and wanted to marry me.

Then I was the happiest girl in the world. We became engaged and decided that right after the wedding we would go to America together. A few weeks passed, and the day of our wedding came.

The guests gathered, the music played gaily, but about an hour before the ceremony my bridegroom called me in to another room and told me he couldn't marry me, because he didn't want to make me unhappy. He explained it was all a mistake on his part, because he couldn't forget his sweetheart. I didn't know what hit me, I began to cry and plead with him to have pity on me and not shame me so. But he was adamant. Since I thought that his sweetheart was in America, I promised him that, if he found her, I would release him. He grasped my hands and kissed them, and after that we went through with the ceremony.

A few weeks after the wedding we left. My aunt, who met us in America, greeted us warmly, and my uncle found a good job for my husband. My husband loved me honestly, and of course I loved him, and we lived together happily almost three years, but after that came my misfortune.

I had noticed, weeks ago, that he was upset. My heart told me then that trouble was brewing. He went about sadly, and I heard him sighing and groaning. He started coming home late and didn't even go over to our baby, whom he loves very much.

I finally asked him what had happened to him. He looked at me. He asked me if I remembered what I had promised him before the wedding. When I heard those words I fainted and was sick for several days. When I felt better he talked to me and, with tears in his eyes, begged me to calm down, because there was no other way out.

He explained that since he had just met his sweetheart, who had been in America all the time, he no longer belonged to me but to her. He says he will leave me our home, his money, and will pay me alimony too. But we must part. I fell at his feet, cried, and begged him to have pity on me and our young child, but he had one answer: "It can't be any other way."

I beg you, have mercy on me. My husband is a good man with a fine character, and he is a faithful reader of the *Forward*.

Write a few words to him in your answer to my letter. How can he demand of me that I set him free? The truth is that when I made him that promise I never believed he would ever find his sweetheart.

I wait with greatest impatience to see my letter and your answer printed.

Thank you in advance,
Heartbroken

ANSWER:

The man has no right to leave his wife now, after he lived with her for three happy years and has a child with her. Even though his wife promised him before the wedding that she would free him, he dare not demand now that she keep her word. If he is really a decent man with a good heart and fine character, he must understand that he now has more obligation to his wife and child than to that sweetheart who vanished for years and didn't concern herself about him.

1907

Worthy Mr. Editor,

I am a workingman, and two years ago I entered into a partnership with another worker. We took in several other people, whom we paid well, and we all earned good wages.

During the two years we worked together, I was sick for three weeks, but my partner, who worked with the whole "set" of workers, gave me the usual half of the profits. I didn't want to take it, since I hadn't worked, but my partner, an honorable man, brought me the entire half.

Some time ago my partner got sick, and the first two weeks, I, too, gave him half of what we earned. But when I wanted to give him his share after the third week, he didn't want to take it. He explained to me then that the partnership would have to be dissolved because his doctor had told him to stop working. I had to agree to it.

Now my former partner has a small business, but he is not doing well. I, on the contrary, have worked a full season with the whole "set" and earned a great deal.

My question now is whether I have any obligations to my former partner, because since he became sick and left me I am earning more than usual. I want to remark that I am a family man with young children, but I don't want to take what belongs to another. If you, Mr. Editor, will tell me I have a duty toward him, I will fulfill it.

My former partner is a very decent man, and when I go into his house and see his need, my heart aches. I imagine that he would deal better with me in such a situation. I even loaned him three hundred dollars for his business, which he'll surely repay, but that's a separate matter.

I thank you in advance for your good advice.

Respectfully,
A Reader

ANSWER:
It is comforting to see that there is still compassion in the world. According to the official rule of "mine" and "thine," the writer of the letter, after the partnership was dissolved, owes his partner nothing at all. But according to a rule of human kindness, he should give any and all help with an open hand to this faithful and honorable friend.

1907

Worthy Editor,

I was born in America and my parents gave me a good education. I studied Yiddish and Hebrew, finished high school, completed a course in bookkeeping and got a good job. I have many friends, and several boys have already proposed to me.

Recently I went to visit my parents' home town in Russian Poland. My mother's family in Europe had invited my parents to a wedding, but instead of going themselves, they sent me. I stayed at my grandmother's with an aunt and uncle and had a good time. Our European family, like my parents, are quite well off and they treated me well. They indulged me in everything and I stayed with them six months.

It was lively in the town. There were many organizations and clubs and they all accepted me warmly, looked up to me— after all, I was a citizen of the free land, America. Among the social leaders of the community was an intelligent young man, a friend of my uncle's, who took me to various gatherings and affairs.

He was very attentive, and after a short while he declared his love for me in a long letter. I had noticed that he was not indifferent to me, and I liked him as well. I looked up to him and respected him, as did all the townsfolk. My family became aware of it, and when they spoke to me about him, I could see they thought it was a good match.

He was handsome, clever, educated, a good talker and charmed me, but I didn't give him a definite answer. As my love for him grew, however, I wrote to my parents about him, and then we became officially engaged.

A few months later we both went to my parents in the States and they received him like their own son. My bridegroom immediately began to learn English and tried to adjust to the new life. Yet when I introduced him to my friends they looked at him with disappointment. "This 'greenhorn' is your fiancé?" they asked. I told them what a big role he played in his town, how everyone respected him, but they looked at me as if I were crazy and scoffed at my words.

At first I thought, Let them laugh, when they get better acquainted with him they'll talk differently. In time, though,

I was affected by their talk and began to think, like them, that he really was a "greenhorn" and acted like one.

In short, my love for him is cooling off gradually. I'm suffering terribly because my feelings for him are changing. In Europe, where everyone admired him and all the girls envied me, he looked different. But, here, I see before me another person.

I haven't the courage to tell him, and I can't even talk about it to my parents. He still loves me with all his heart, and I don't know what to do. I choke it all up inside myself, and I beg you to help me with advice in my desperate situation.

Respectfully,
A Worried Reader

ANSWER:

The writer would make a grave mistake if she were to separate from her bridegroom now. She must not lose her common sense and be influenced by the foolish opinions of her friends who divided the world into "greenhorns" and real Americans.

We can assure the writer that her bridegroom will learn English quickly. He will know American history and literature as well as her friends do, and be a better American than they. She should be proud of his love and laugh at those who call him "greenhorn."

1907

Worthy Editor,

Allow me a little space in your newspaper and, I beg you, give me some advice as to what to do.

There are seven people in our family—parents and five children. I am the oldest child, a fourteen-year-old girl. We have been in the country two years and my father, who is a frail man, is the only one working to support the whole family.

I go to school, where I do very well. But since times are hard now and my father earned only five dollars this week, I began to talk about giving up my studies and going to work in order to help my father as much as possible. But my mother didn't even want to hear of it. She wants me to continue my education. She even went out and spent ten dollars on winter clothes for me. But I didn't enjoy the clothes, because I think I am doing the wrong thing. Instead of bringing something into the house, my parents have to spend money on me.

I have a lot of compassion for my parents. My mother is now pregnant, but she still has to take care of the three boarders we have in the house. Mother and Father work very hard and they want to keep me in school.

I am writing to you without their knowledge, and I beg you to tell me how to act. Hoping you can advise me, I remain,

Your reader,
S.

ANSWER:

The advice to the girl is that she should obey her parents and further her education, because in that way she will be able to give them greater satisfaction than if she went out to work.

The hunger for education was very great among the East Side Jews from Eastern Europe. Immigrant mothers who couldn't speak English went to the library and held up the fingers of their hand to indicate the number of children they had. They then would get a card, give it to each of their children, and say, "Go, learn, read."

I graduated from P.S. 20 with George Gershwin, Edward G. Robinson, Paul Muni and Senator Jacob Javits, all sons of immigrants.

1907

Dear Editor,

I am one of those unfortunate girls thrown by fate into a dark and dismal shop, and I need your counsel.

Along with my parents, sisters and brothers, I came from Russian Poland where I had been well educated. But because of the terrible things going on in Russia we were forced to emigrate to America. I am now seventeen years old, but I look younger and they say I am attractive.

A relative talked us into moving to Vineland, New Jersey, and here in this small town I went to work in a shop. In this shop there is a foreman who is an exploiter, and he sets prices on the work. He figures it out so that the wages are very low, he insults and reviles the workers, he fires them and then takes them back. And worse than all of this, in spite of the fact that he has a wife and several children, he often allows himself to "have fun" with some of the working girls. It was my bad luck to be one of the girls that he tried to make advances to. And woe to any girl who doesn't willingly accept them.

Though my few hard-earned dollars mean a lot to my family of eight souls, I didn't want to accept the foreman's vulgar advances. He started to pick on me, said my work was no good, and when I proved to him he was wrong, he started to shout at me in the vilest language. He insulted me in Yiddish and then in English, so the American workers could understand too. Then, as if the Devil were after me, I ran home.

I am left without a job. Can you imagine my circumstances and that of my parents who depend on my earnings? The girls in the shop were very upset over the foreman's vulgarity but they don't want him to throw them out, so they are afraid to be witnesses against him. What can be done about this? I beg you to answer me.

Respectfully,
A Shopgirl

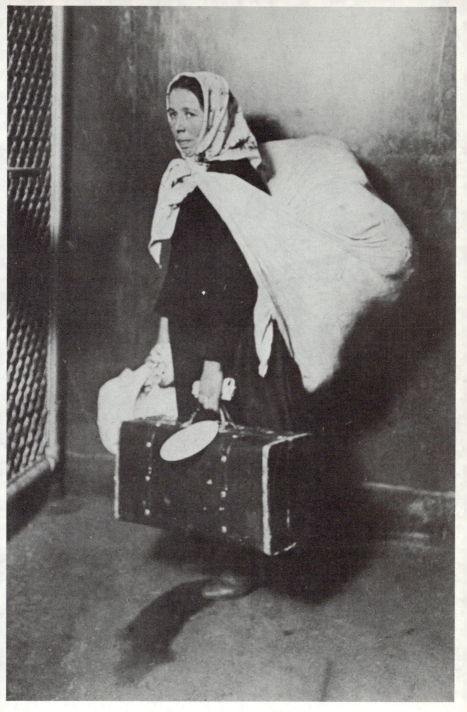

Slovak woman, Ellis Island, 1905.

Immigrants on an Atlantic liner to New York, 1906.

Jewish immigrant in New York, 1915.

A grandmother at Ellis Island, 1924.

Laundry drying on the Lower East Side, c. 1900.

Newsboys under the arch of Brooklyn Bridge, c. 1912.

A typical market scene in Lower New York City, c. 1900.

Shopping on Hester Street, 1895.

Lower East Side tenement kitchen, 1915.

ANSWER:

Such a scoundrel should be taught a lesson that could be an example to others. The girl is advised to bring out into the open the whole story about the foreman, because there in the small town it shouldn't be difficult to have him thrown out of the shop and for her to get her job back.

1908

Dear Editor,

I ask you to give me some advice in my situation.

I am a young man of twenty-five, sixteen years in America, and I recently met a fine girl. She has a flaw, however, that keeps me from marrying her. The fault is that she has a dimple in her chin, and it is said that people who have this lose their first husband or wife.

At first I laughed at the idea, but later it began to bother me. I began to observe people with dimpled chins and found out that their first husbands or wives really had died prematurely. I got so interested in this that whenever I see someone with this defect I ask about it immediately, and I find out that some of the men have lost their first wives, and some of the women's first husbands are dead.

This upset me so that I don't know what to do. I can't leave my sweetheart. I love her very much. Bur I'm afraid to marry her lest I die because of the dimple. I've questioned many people. Some say it's true, others laugh at the idea.

Perhaps you, too, will laugh at me for being such a fool and believing such nonsense, but I cannot rest until I hear your opinion about it. I want to add that my sweetheart knows nothing about this.

Respectfully,
The Unhappy Fool

ANSWER:

The tragedy is not that the girl has a dimple in her chin but that some people have a screw loose in their heads! One would need the knowledge of a genius to explain how a dimple in the chin could drive a husband or wife to the grave. Does the angel of death sit hiding in the dimple? It seems to us that it is a beauty spot, and we never imagined it could house the Devil!

It's tragic humor to find such superstition in the world today. It's truly shameful that a young man who was brought up in America should ask such questions. To calm him, we wish to tell him we know many people with such dimples who have not lost their first husbands or wives, but live out their years together in great happiness.

1908

Worthy Mr. Editor,

Please help us decide who is right in the debate between friends, whether a Socialist and freethinker should observe *yohrzeit?*

Among the disputants there is a Socialist, a freethinker, who observes his mother's *yohrzeit* in the following manner: He pays a pious man to say the *kaddish* prayer for the dead, and burns a *yohrzeit* candle in his home. He himself doesn't say *kaddish*, because he doesn't believe in religion. But his desire to respect the memory of his mother is so strong that it does not prevent him from performing this religious ceremony.

Among the debaters there are those who do not want to know of such an emotion as honoring the dead. But if one does desire to do so, one should say *kaddish* himself, even if he does not believe in it.

Therefore, our first question is: Can we recognize the beautiful human emotion of honoring the dead, especially when it concerns one so near as a mother? The second question: If so, should the expression of honor be in keeping with the desires of the honored? Third: Would it be more conscientious and righteous if the freethinker said *kaddish* himself, or if he hired a pious man to do it for him?

Being convinced that this matter interests a great number of people, we hope you, Mr. Editor, will answer us soon.

With regards,
The Debating Group

ANSWER:

Honoring a departed one who was cherished and loved is a gracious sentiment and a requisite for the living. And everyone wants to be remembered after his death. Socialists and freethinkers observe the anniversaries of their great leaders—just recently they commemorated the twenty-fifth anniversary of the death of Karl Marx.

Saying *kaddish* is certainly a religious rite, and to pay someone to say *kiddish* is not the act of a freethinker. But we can understand the psychology of a freethinker who feels that hiring someone else is not as much against his own convictions as to say *kaddish* himself.

My father was a Socialist and a freethinker, but he went to shul *every Friday night and Saturday and attended the synagogue on every holiday and every ceremonial. Once when I chided him about his piety in view of the fact that he was a freethinker, he answered me, "These people are my brethren, they are the people among whom I was raised, and I love them. Dudja Silverberg* [a very pious Jew] *goes to* shul *to speak with God, I go to* shul *to speak with Dudja."*

1908

My dearest friends of the *Forward,*

I appeal to you for help, since I have no better comrades than the workers.

I have been jobless for six months now. I have eaten the last shirt on my back and now there is nothing left for me but to end my life. I have struggled long enough in the dark world. Death is better than such a life. One goes about with strong hands, one wants to sell them for a bit of bread, and no one wants to buy. They tell you cold-bloodedly: "We don't need you." Can you imagine how heartsick one gets?

I get up at four in the morning to hunt a job through the newspaper. I have no money for carfare, so I go on foot, but by the time I get to the place there are hundreds before me. Then I run wherever my eyes lead me. Lately I've spent five cents a day on food, and the last two days I don't have even that. I have no strength to go on.

I am an ironworker. I can work a milling machine and a drill press. I can also drive horses and train colts. In Russia I served in the cavalry, and there I once hit my superior. For that I was sent to prison for forty days. Then I was returned to my squadron and my case was transferred to the military court in Kiev. Then orders came for me to be brought to Kiev.

When I learned of this I fled at three o'clock in the morning. I gave my gun and sword to the Bund organization and they gave me passage money to America.

If I had known it would be so bitter for me here, I wouldn't have come. I didn't come here for a fortune, but where is bread? What can I do now? I ask you, comrades. I beg you to help me in my dire need. Do not let a man die a horrible death.

Your friend,
G.B.
[Full name and address were given]

ANSWER:

This is one of hundreds of heartrending pleas for help, cries of need, that we receive daily. The writer of this letter is told to go first to the Crisis Conference at 133 Eldridge Street, New York, and they will not let him starve. And further we ask our readers to let us know if someone can create a job for this unemployed man.

1908

Dear Mr. Editor,

If anyone had ever told me that I would someday write to the "Bintel Brief" I would have laughed at him. Things are going well for me. I make a living, I have no wife with boarders and I am not in love yet. I have never done anyone a wrong that would be on my conscience. And yet I come to you for advice.

I am a barber and have been practicing the "art" for ten years and became quite adept at it. Sounds good, yes? But the following happened:

A few weeks ago, on a quiet afternoon when there were no customers and the boss was out somewhere, I dozed off while reading the *Police Gazette*. And I soon dreamed that a customer entered. The boss and I took our positions near our chairs, and as usual the customer selected the one manned by my boss. As usual, I was a bit insulted as a craftsman, and a little vexed over being robbed of the tip. But it happened that the boss was called away in a hurry and he asked me to tend to the customer. I began to work on him and he laughed in my face. He grimaced, made strange faces, stuck out his tongue at me, and began to yell. And though I didn't understand the language, I felt he was calling me a clumsy barber.

My patience finally gave out. And as I held the razor in my hand (don't question a dream!), I slit his throat. So naturally there was screaming and tumult and I awoke. I spat three times to banish the dream, but it didn't help.

Dear Editor, it must seem strange, or like a story created by a sick imagination, but what I write here is the truth: since my foolish dream, I cannot rest. I can't forget the scene. I am always lost in thought and obsessed with the dream. When I stand at my work and have to use my razor, I get a sudden impulse to do what I did in my dream. The greatest temptation I have to withstand is when my razor gets under the chin close to the neck. Oh, then it's terrible! I am afraid I will go mad. I tried staying home from work two days, but I can't get the thoughts out of my head.

I haven't told anyone about this yet, because I am ashamed. I beg you to advise me what to do. Shall I give up my job? I am willing to do anything to rid myself of my dilemma and my suffering. I beg you to give me your opinion. Isn't it madness?

With greatest respect,
A Mad Barber (?)

ANSWER:

Man's thoughts often weave automatically through "idea-patterns," as they are called in psychological science, and the muscles respond automatically to the ideas. Every man with a healthy will can shake off the unwanted ideas and the reflexes they call forth to the muscles.

Every man can dream he commits a terrible crime, because in dreams the controllable will is slumbering. The writer of this letter must simply laugh off the dream and drive the whole matter out of his head. But if his nervous system is for some reason weakened and therefore his control over his will power likewise weak, he must consult a doctor. But he himself must be strong and overcome his impulse.

1908

Dear Editor,

Recently my wife hired a Jewish servant girl who looked very dejected. We talked with her, asked her what was wrong, and she told us the following story: She comes from Lithuania. She has been in America for three years, has no friends, and worked in one place all these years. She had saved two hundred and fifty dollars which she had kept in Epstein's Bank in Brooklyn. Unfortunately Epstein's Bank closed down a few months ago. She had hoped to save up three hundred dollars and then go home. Now she hasn't a cent.

Unfortunately, we can help her only with comforting words. She goes around worried all the time, and she told my wife that she thinks of suicide. She can't forget her bitter state and says she has no more goals in life. My wife is afraid to send her away, because some evil might befall her.

My wife and I are gentle with her and we try to keep her from worrying. A few days ago a poor man knocked at the door and asked for alms. My wife told the girl to take a penny to him. She took the penny, went to the beggar, and said to him, "Mr. Epstein took all of my money, I have nothing," and fell to the floor in a faint.

My wife was frightened and could hardly bring her to. When she recovered she said to my wife, "I want to go to sleep and never awaken." We are afraid something might happen to our unfortunate girl.

I appeal to you here for advice on how to deal with her. I enclose my name and address.

Respectfully,
S.D.—Brooklyn

ANSWER:

Is it so surprising that this unhappy girl is so shattered? It took her long enough to save up the money. It's a severe blow, and hopefully, goodhearted people could raise at least part of the money for her. Possibly this letter will reach people who are in a position to bring back the will to live to this unfortunate girl. The writer of this letter and his wife must try everything possible to keep this girl with them. Hopefully, time will bring her peace of mind.

1908

Dear Editor,

We are two brothers who live together and have worked together. We earned a living for ourselves and were able to send money to our parents in Europe. But now unfortunately we've been out of work for three months, and we cannot send anything to our parents.

My brother had an idea that we should go to Panama. He heard that workers were being sent there and paid good wages (sixty-five cents an hour). I must say that we love our parents very much, and we would like to be able to save enough money to go home to our poor old mother and father. But I am afraid it's not true that such high wages are paid there.

We are lonely here and we don't know whom to ask and what to do. So we beg you to advise us and answer soon. We thank you in advance.

Your constant readers,
I. Brothers

ANSWER:

There are no honeypots in Panama. The climate is unhealthy, the work is hard, and one lives among all kinds of people, some of them half savage. It's hard to get away from there if one has no money.

But if you cannot help yourself here, and if you are strong and capable of endurance, you can make a few dollars at that work. You can find out how much is being paid there at the office at 74 Lafayette Street, New York.

1908

Worthy Editor,

I have been in America almost three years. I came from Russia where I studied at a *yeshiva*. My parents were proud and happy at the thought that I would become a rabbi. But at the age of twenty I had to go to America. Before I left I gave my father my word that I would walk the righteous path and be good and pious. But America makes one forget everything.

Here I became an operator, and at night I went to school. In a few months I entered a preparatory school, where for two subjects I had a Gentile girl as teacher. I began to notice that the teacher paid more attention to me than to the others in the class and in time she told me I would be better off taking private lessons from her for the same price I paid to the school.

I agreed, and soon realized that her lessons with me were not ordinary. For example, I was to pay five dollars a month for two hours a week, but she gave me three lessons a week, each lasting two and sometimes three hours. Then I had to stop the lessons because I had no money to pay her. However, she wanted to teach me without pay, explaining that she taught not only for money but also because teaching gave her pleasure.

In short, I began to feel at home in her house and not only she but also her parents welcomed me warmly. I ate there often and they also lent me money when I was in need. I used to ask myself, "What am I doing? but I couldn't help myself.

There was a depression at the time, I had no job and had to accept their aid.

I don't know what I would have done without her help. I began to love her, but with mixed feelings of respect and anguish. I was afraid to look her in the eyes. I looked at her like a Russian soldier looks at his superior officer and I never imagined she thought of marrying me.

A few weeks ago I took the Regents examinations for entering college. After the exams, my teacher told me not to look for work for a few weeks, but to eat and drink at their home. I didn't want to but she insisted and I couldn't refuse.

Many times upon leaving her house, I would decide not to return, but my heart drew me to her, and I spent three weeks in her house. Meanwhile I received the report on my examinations which showed that I had passed with the highest grades. I went directly to her to show her the report and she asked me what I planned to do. I answered that I didn't know as yet, because I had no money for college. "That's a minor problem," she said, and asked if I didn't know that she was not indifferent toward me. Then she spoke frankly of her love for me and her hope that I would love her.

"If you are not against it, my parents and I will support you while you study. The fact that I am a Gentile and you a Jew should not bother us. We are both, first of all, human beings and we will live as such." She told me she believed that all men and all nations were equal.

I was confused and I couldn't answer her immediately. In Europe I had been absorbed in the *yeshiva*, here with my studies, and I knew little of practical life. I do agree with her that we are first of all human beings, and she is a human being in the fullest sense of the word. She is pretty, intelligent, educated, and has a good character. But I am in despair when I think of my parents. What heartaches they will have when they learn of this!

I asked her to give me a few days to think it over. I go around confused and yet I am drawn to her. I must see her every day, but when I am there I think of my parents and I am torn by doubt.

I wait impatiently for your answer.

Respectfully,
Skeptic from Philadelphia

ANSWER:

We can only say that some mixed marriages are happy, others unhappy. But then many marriages between Jew and Jew, Christian and Christian, are not successful either. It is true, however, that in some mixed marriages the differences between man and wife create unhappiness. Therefore we cannot take it upon ourselves to advise the young man regarding this marriage. This he must decide for himself.

1908

Worthy Editor,

Have pity on me and my two small children and print my letter in the *Forward*.

Max! The children and I now say farewell to you. You left us in such a terrible state. You had no compassion for us. For six years I loved you faithfully, took care of you like a loyal servant, never had a happy day with you. Yet I forgive you for everything.

Have you ever asked yourself why you left us? Max, where is your conscience: you used to have sympathy for the forsaken women and used to say their terrible plight was due to the men who left them in dire need. And how did you act? I was a young, educated, decent girl when you took me. You lived with me for six years, during which time I bore you four children. And then you left me.

Of the four children, only two remain, but you have made

them living orphans. Who will bring them up? Who will support us? Have you no pity for your own flesh and blood? Consider what you are doing. My tears choke me and I cannot write any more.

Be advised that in several days I am leaving with my two living orphans for Russia. We say farewell to you and beg you to take pity on us and send us enough to live on. My address in Russia will be ―――― [Full name and address were given].

Your Deserted Wife and Children

The most dreaded word in the Yiddish language is agunah *a deserted wife. The Jewish Daily Forward at one time ran a regular feature seeking husbands who had deserted their wives, and the Jewish Information Agency of New York also had a bureau seeking deserting husbands. It was a very sad thing, especially when the wife had been left with two or three children and no income.*

1908

Esteemed Editor,

We were sitting in the shop and working when the boss came over to one of us and said, "You ruined the work: you'll have to pay for it." The worker answered that it wasn't his fault, that he had given out the work in perfect condition. "You're trying to tell me!" The boss got mad and began to shout. "I pay your wages and you answer back, you dog! I should have thrown you out of my shop long ago."

The worker trembled, his face got whiter. When the boss noticed how his face paled, he gestured, spat and walked away. The worker said no more. Tired, and overcome with shame, he turned back to his work and later he exclaimed, "For six years I've been working here like a slave, and he tells me, 'You dog, I'll throw you out!' I wanted to pick up an iron and smash his head in, but I saw before me my wife and five children who want to eat!"

Obviously, the offended man felt he had done wrong in not standing up for his honor as a worker and human being. In the shop, the machines hummed, the irons thumped, and we could see the tears running down his cheeks.

Did this unfortunate man act correctly in remaining silent under the insults of the boss? Is the fact that he has a wife and children the reason for his slavery and refusal to defend himself? I hope you will answer my questions in the "Bintel Brief."

Respectfully,
A.P.

ANSWER:

The worker cannot help himself alone. There is no limit to what must be done for a piece of bread. One must bite his lips till they bleed, and keep silent when he is alone. But he must not remain alone. He must not remain silent. He must unite with his fellow workers and fight. To defend their honor as men, the workers must be well organized.

1908

Dear Mr. Editor,

I am an unhappy lonely orphan, fifteen years of age, and I appeal to you in my helplessness.

My story is a tragic one. Fifteen years ago when there was a depression in the country, my parents lived in Boston, and there I was born. My father was an operator, and at that time he was out of a job for a long time. At home we were starving for a piece of bread, but my mother wouldn't go to strangers to beg because she was ashamed. She had come from a rich family in Europe.

On a certain morning, when my mother went out into the

hall she found food that good people had left at our door. That same day, from misery and shame, she killed herself by slitting her throat with a knife. I was five months old at the time and was one of the three children that she left.

After my mother's death, my father placed my brother and sister in an orphanage and sent me to a wet nurse. When my mother's father learned of the tragedy he came to America to take us, the three orphans, to his home in Bialystok. My father, however, refused to give up all of the children and told him he could only take me. At that time I was nine months old. Having no alternative, my grandfather took me, alone, to Europe.

I was brought up by my grandfather and grandmother as their own child, called them Mother and Father, and knew nothing of my past. When I was older, I saw my grandfather lighting a large candle one evening and placing it on the buffet. I asked him what it meant and then he told me, "This is a *yohrzeit* candle for your mother." I was shocked, and when I began to ask questions, Grandmother began to cry and told me everything. Then grandfather brought out a large picture of my mother and father, with my sister and brother.

From that time on I went about heavy-hearted and had one thought in mind, to meet my father, brother and sister for whom I longed. And so a few years passed. Then my grandmother fell sick and passed away.

My grandfather didn't wait long, but married a second time. This opened a new well of troubles for me. My stepmother began to persecute me and my aunt, a single girl, who also lived with Grandfather. My aunt couldn't stand it and Grandfather gave her money to go to America. When I remained alone, my stepmother vented all her hatred on me. She didn't give me enough to eat and many times she chased me out of the house. Strangers used to take me in and feed me. My grandfather was helpless and couldn't do anything against the woman. Thus I struggled for a time till my aunt in America had mercy on me. She bought a steamship ticket on the installment plan and sent for me.

Now I am fifteen years old and I've been here in the country for five months. I do not work and I haven't earned a penny. My aunt supports me, but I can't stand watching her struggles. She works very hard in order to keep me with her. Whenever I go to look for work they tell me they do not need me.

I don't know what to do and I turn to you, honored Editor. I beg you to publish my letter. Maybe someone will turn up who knows about my father, my brother and sister. When the tragedy occurred, my father lived in Boston, at ———. [In the letter the girl gives her name and address, and the names of her father, brother and sister.] I thank you in advance for printing my letter.

The Lonesome Orphan,
N.M.

ANSWER:

Soon after the letter from the Lonesome Orphan was published, many letters were printed in the *Forward* from people who offered to help the girl. Some were prepared to take her into their homes as their own child, others wanted to assist her financially.

1908

Dear Editor,

I am one of those unfortunates who for many years has suffered from the worker's disease. The times and the conditions have taught me to be patient and to endure the pain.

I am the father of a three-year-old girl, a clever, pretty child who attracts everyone's attention. All who know my child hug her and kiss her. But I may not. I know this all too well, yet I can't keep myself from kissing my little girl. Every time I hold the child in my arms and kiss her, my conscience bothers me. I promise myself that I will not do it again, but I can't overcome my weakness. This bothers me more than the suffering from consumption, because I know I am infecting my innocent child.

Every time I kiss the child I feel my wife's eyes on me, as if she wanted to shout, "Murderer!" but she doesn't utter a word—only her face reddens. I feel, then, that a battle is going on within her; she compresses her lips and remains silent. She tries to keep the child away from me though she doesn't want to hurt me. My wife's suffering just deepens my pain.

What can I do when I cannot control myself? I beg you to advise me how to act. Thank you in advance,

An Unhappy Father

ANSWER:

It's heartbreaking for us to have to tell this unhappy father: Control yourself and do not kiss your dear child. This is the only advice we can give him. He must discipline himself. The father could live a long life with his ailment. With good treatment, consumptives can live out their years, and he might yet live to have a lot of pleasure from his little daughter.

The workman's disease was tuberculosis, endemic on the East Side during the sweatshop era. A Verein doctor would call on the sick man and look around his house of three children and his pregnant wife and what could he tell him? Could he tell the workingman to go to Colorado? With what money? So the best he could do was prescribe some cough medicine and tell the man to rest as much as possible. One doctor used to write on the prescription slip, "Join the Cloakmakers Union."

1908

Worthy Editor,

Allow me a little space in the "Bintel Brief" to write about something that happened to me.

I worked for the Police Department for a year. My job was to trail thieves, pickpockets, and gather evidence against brothels. The state paid me seventy dollars a month, and my record for the year was very good. My boss, Officer Bingham, was very pleased with me, and took me in to work at headquarters. I worked there two months and caught twelve robbers red-handed. Then hear what happened:

A complaint came in to headquarters that a certain restaurant was selling liquor without a license and I was sent to investigate. I came into the restaurant, sat down at a table, and read the *Forward*. Soon a man came over to me, and I ordered a complete dinner and a *schnapps*. I finished the meal, the drink, paid the sum of eighteen cents to the man, and looked around. I saw the owner's seven children with their pale, emaciated mother, and I felt I could not be so heartless as to take the father away from them since I knew he would be sent to the City Jail for one hundred and twenty days. I saw, too, that he certainly didn't have six hundred dollars to pay the fine.

Well, I showed him the complaint letter and warned him to stop selling liquor. He thanked me and wanted to give me five dollars, but I wouldn't take it.

When I returned to the station I told the lieutenant who questioned me that there was no liquor or beer there. But the lieutenant decided to send me to the restaurant with a man who had worked there as a waiter and he would show me where the liquor was kept. So I had to go back to the restaurant with the waiter. On the way I asked him why he had squealed on such a poor man. His answer was that the boss owed him four dollars and didn't want to pay.

Well, I came into the restaurant with the waiter, I winked at the owner and asked for a *schnapps*. When he answered that he didn't sell whiskey, the waiter ran over to the counter, grabbed a bottle of whiskey and showed it to me. I told the waiter then that he could have whiskey there but was not allowed to sell it. I advised the owner to pay the waiter the four dollars, which he did. When we got outside I told the waiter he should be ashamed of himself for squealing. We had an argument and I slapped him around a little.

Later, when we got to the police station, I was called into the captain's office, and he told me I was fired. I said good-by and good luck and left. A few days later the captain called me back, but I told him I didn't want to do that kind of work any longer. They are after me to come back, and I could now get seventy-five and maybe eighty dollars a month. But I don't want to.

I must add here that I am not a real police detective, because I don't wear a badge, and that's because I am not yet twenty-one years old.

I don't want to go back because I haven't the heart to see a poor man punished for selling a glass of whiskey for three cents. I would rather starve than send such a man to prison. I told this to the captain, and remarked that there are millionaires who commit greater crimes and get away with them. Some real detectives told me I handled the situation with the restaurant owner correctly, and that they wouldn't have the heart to arrest him either.

Now I ask you to advise me what I should do. I will do what you tell me. I have taken a dislike to the job, and if times weren't so bad now, I wouldn't even consider going back.

> Respectfully,
> Former Assistant Detective

ANSWER:

In the answer, the young assistant-detective is praised for his actions, for not wanting to inform on a poor man. The advice to him is to run from the job as from a fire, because this work is not fit for such a fine kindhearted young man. It is not right to place himself in servitude to the Police Department. There is the danger that he might, in time, not be able to withstand temptation and it would be hard to guard himself against sinking into the corruption of immoral police practice.

1909

Worthy Editor,

I find myself in such a situation that I need your advice. I am one of the immigrant shopgirls, twenty years old, and I earn a decent living.

A short time ago I became acquainted with a young man who goes to a preparatory school and wants to become a doctor. He came to my house many times to visit, but as time went on I began to fall in love with him. He also declared his love for me, and that's when my trouble began.

Six months ago I received a letter from my parents, in which they propose a match for me with one of our relatives who is also in America. He does not live in New York. I don't know the boy, but we correspond and have sent each other photographs. We liked each other from the pictures, and I know that he is a businessman and makes a decent living. But my heart draws me to the other boy.

Honorable Editor, tell me what to do. My friends have tried to talk me out of tying myself down to work for seven years to help my friend through his studies. I would be twenty-seven years old then and I will have lost the bloom of youth after seven years of toil in the shop. That is why I worry about my future.

How shall I solve this problem? Shall I refuse him and try to forget him? Whatever you advise me, I will do.

Your constant reader,
A.B.

ANSWER:

After years of study many such young students often fall out of love and leave the girls who have helped them. A graduate doctor doesn't want to marry a toilworn old maid. She has worked her fingers to the bone and exhausted herself to help him become

"Sir Doctor." All that can be said to him when he leaves her is "You should be ashamed of yourself, Sir Doctor." But one cannot generalize and say that all young men who complete their education act this way. It may be possible that the letter writer's friend is different. However, it is hard to judge, and therefore difficult to advise the writer how to act. She must make her own decision in this matter.

1909

Dear Editor,

As a reader of the *Forward*, I am writing to you about a matter that will interest other people too. But first I will tell you a little about myself.

I am twenty-seven years of age, have been in the country ten years, and am still single. I have worked here at various trades, but never very long at one job. I enjoy traveling and seeing what's going on in the country. Now I've decided it's time to marry and settle down.

I came to North Dakota, where most people make their living from farming. But there are no Jews in this area. I started to work on a farm and I learned farming. I like this kind of life, and after working a year and a half I rented a farm for myself.

My capital was small, but Gentile neighbors helped me. I went into debt for thirteen hundred dollars, but by the end of the summer I had paid back almost all of my debts. I wrote to a friend of mine about joining me. He and his wife came and we work together. We carry on an independent life, have none of the problems of city life because we always have our own potatoes, butter, cheese, milk, chickens, a good home and are content.

This winter I went to Chicago and stayed a few weeks with friends. Most of my friends called me an idiot and told me they could not understand how a young, capable fellow like me became a farmer and leads such a lonely life.

Of all the girls I knew, who would have gladly married me before, not one was interested in going back to the farm with me. But this didn't discourage me. I returned to the farm and I'm now preparing for the spring season.

However, I want to ask you, did my friends have the right to call me "idiot"? Is there any logic in their argument? Please answer me.

Thank you,
The Jewish Farmer

ANSWER:
There is certainly nothing to be ashamed of in living in the lap of Nature. Many people dream of becoming farmers. The cities are full of many diseases that are unheard of on farms. Tuberculosis, for instance, is a disease of the big cities. People in urban areas grow old and gray at forty, but most of the farmers are healthy and strong and live to be eighty and ninety.

Generally, it is a matter of choice. Debates between country people and city people about which have the better life are nothing new.

1909

Dear Mr. Editor,

I am a young man of twenty-two and have every reason to be happy, but I am unhappy because nature saw fit to give me red hair. Because of the color of my hair, I endure many insults in the shop and on the street. When I hear someone say to me, "Hello, Red!" I am hurt and offended.

I am unhappy and lonely, and I've even consulted doctors about it. One of them advised me to dye my hair. Another told me not to do it because, first of all, it has a bad effect on the scalp, and, secondly, the color would not be natural.

I would be very thankful to you if you could advise me in this situation.

Respectfully,
Unhappy

ANSWER:

A person is not valued by the hair on his head but by what is in his head. Those who laugh at this young man's red hair have no brains and he should not be disturbed over their stupidity. He has more reason to laugh at their heads, which are empty.

If an intelligent person greets him occasionally with a "Hello, Red," he means no harm. The same one would greet a blonde with "Hello, Blondie!" The letter writer has absolutely no reason to be upset about this.

1909

Worthy Editor,

I often spend time with a group of forty people, thirty men and ten women. Among them are religious and non-religious people, and we do not pass the time in idle discussions.

Recently we read a report in a newspaper about the movement to give women the right to vote, and for the past few weeks we have been carrying on a debate about it. I am one of the group that is in favor of giving women full rights, but most of the others are against it. The opposed argue that it would be very bad to let the women get to the ballot box, because that would destroy their family life. The woman would then no longer be the housewife, the mother to her children, the wife to her husband—in a word, everything would be destroyed.

A woman must not mix in politics, they say. She was created to be dependent on man, obey him, love him, supply all his comforts and be a mother to his children. The question arises: Must the woman then be considered a slave, and the man the master? Isn't it obvious, then, that women in many cases show themselves to be cleverer than men? These same people who recently celebrated the hundredth birthday of Abraham Lincoln, for having freed the Negro slaves, now talk with a satirical grin about women's freedom. Just as the opponents of the Socialist movement point out that Socialism will be harmful, so those who argue against voting rights for women say that this will destroy family life.

This is not so, because a woman is a human being just like a man. The capabilities that women have already shown confirm this. Plenty of facts can be cited from the past. And if women are recognized as human beings, they must also be granted all the rights of human beings. I think that if women are considered human beings with all their rights, then family life would be better and richer.

> With Socialistic regards,
> L.V.

ANSWER:
The arguments against the opponents of women's rights are very good ones. The fact is that many intelligent women are already taking part in various activities and they still remain excellent homemakers.

Justice can reign among people only when they all have equal rights. If one has more power than the other, it leads to injustice. Those men who are opposed to giving women the same rights they possess are acting from tyrannical instincts because they actually want to rule the women.

1909

Dear Editor,

I come from a small town in Russia. I was brought up by decent parents and got a good education. I am now twenty years old and am a customer-peddler in a Southern city. Since my customers here are colored people, I became acquainted with a young Negro girl, twenty-two years of age, who buys merchandise from me. She is light-skinned and a fine girl. She is a teacher, a graduate of a Negro college, and I think she is an honorable person.

I fell in love with the girl but I couldn't go around with her openly because I am white and she is colored. However, whenever I delivered her order, I visited with her for a while.

In time she went away to another city to teach, and I corresponded with her. When she came home for Christmas, I told her I loved her and I intended to marry her and take her North to live. But she refused me and gave me no reason. Perhaps it was because I am a white man.

I spoke about my love for her to my friends, who are supposedly decent people, and they wanted to spit in my face! They told me openly that if not for my good character they would have nothing to do with me because of "criminal" behavior. To them it appeared that I was about to commit a crime.

Therefore I would like to hear your answer as to whether I should be condemned for falling in love with a Negro woman and wanting to marry her. And if you can, explain to me also her reason for refusing me.

Respectfully,
Z.B.

ANSWER:

It is unthinkable to regard the writer's actions as criminal. But the fact is that in the South the whites have such a deep hatred for the Negroes that when a white man falls in love with a Negro woman it is considered a crime. Many of the Southerners, however, are hypocrites in this respect, because when the Negroes were their slaves, some of the black women bore their children.

Concerning the question as to why the Negro girl refused him and didn't want to marry him: either she does not love him, or this reflects the justly deserved distrust of the Negroes for the whites in the South.

The Jewish peddler was the first friend the Negro of the South had after he was freed. Christian stores did not permit the Negro to try on any of the merchandise: "Nigger, don't touch unless you buy." The Jewish peddler permitted the black lady to try on the dress and the coat and the man to try on the suit. He was also the first white man to sell to the Negro on credit. A Jew was the first white man to sell the Negro an insurance policy. Elderly Negro women have told me how, when the "Jew collector man" came around, they called all the children to see their name on the top of the sheet: "Mr. and Mrs. Jones and family."

1909

Dear Editor,

We, the undersigned, appeal to you to use your worthy newspaper to help save a family from going under.

This is about a family from Yekaterinaslav, Russia, who suffered greatly from the pogroms. The father and a child were murdered, the mother was crippled, a twenty-year-old boy had his head split open, and a sixteen-year-old boy had his arm broken.

The survivors of the family, the mother and three children, came to America, and lived in New Britain, Connecticut. Here the mother was forced to place one child in a Catholic orphanage and give the other two to good people. The older boy, whose head had been split by the hoodlums, had a recurrence of the effects of the blow and was taken into government hospital in New York for cure. Then the authorities decided that he has to be sent back to Russia—to the city where his father and brother had been murdered. His crippled mother intends to go with him, but she is desolate because she has to leave the other children behind.

What will become of this unfortunate's children who remain alone in New Britain? What will happen to the child in the Catholic orphanage? We appeal to all Yekaterinaslaver societies and individuals to help save this family. The boy has been in the country over two years and something must be done to stop his being sent back. If this can't be done, it must at least be made possible for the mother and son to leave the country with a little money for the first piece of bread, because they don't have a red cent.

The boy is in the Staten Island Hospital and will be sent away any day now. *Landsleit* and friends, do your duty to this family that is so alone [here the name of the woman is given].

> With friendly regards,
> Your Readers from New Britain, Connecticut.*

ANSWER:

In this answer it is stated that a reporter from the *Forward* visited the family and verified that the condition was even worse than was described in the letter.

In the answer, the Jews and Jewish organizations are scolded for neglecting these victims of the pogrom for so long, and for not seeing to it that the child was at least placed in a Jewish orphanage. Attention is also called to all those active in Jewish organizations and to the Hebrew Immigrant Aid Society. They can still influence the authorities to keep the young man from being sent back. The Jewish welfare organization and the family's *landsleit* are ordered to act immediately on this case to help the unfortunates.

1909

Dear Editor,

We, the unfortunates who are imprisoned on Ellis Island, beg you to have pity on us and print our letter in your worthy news-

* The above letter is signed by four men.

paper, so that our brothers in America may know how we suffer here.

The people here are from various countries, most of them are Russian Jews, many of whom can never return to Russia. These Jews are deserters from the Russian army and political escapees, whom the Czar would like to have returned to Russia. Many of the families sold everything they owned to scrape together enough for passage to America. They haven't a cent but they figured that, with the help of their children, sisters, brothers and friends, they could find means of livelihood in America.

You know full well how much the Jewish immigrant suffers till he gets to America. First he has a hard enough time at the borders, then with the agents. After this he goes through a lot till they send him, like baggage, on the train to a port. There he lies around in the immigrant sheds till the ship finally leaves. Then follows the torment on the ship, where every sailor considers a steerage passenger a dog. And when, with God's help, he has endured all this, and he is at last in America, he is given for "dessert" an order that he must show that he possesses twenty-five dollars.

But where can we get it? Who ever heard of such an outrage, treating people so? If we had known before, we would have provided for it somehow back at home. What nonsense this is! We must have the money on arrival, yet a few hours later (when relatives come) it's too late. For this kind of nonsense they ruin so many people and send them back to the place they escaped from.

It is impossible to describe all that is taking place here, but we want to convey at least a little of it. We are packed into a room where there is space for two hundred people, but they have crammed in about a thousand. They don't let us out into the yard for a little fresh air. We lie about on the floor in the spittle and filth. We're wearing the same shirts for three or four weeks, because we don't have our baggage with us.

Everyone goes around dejected and cries and wails. Women with little babies, who have come to their husbands, are being detained. Who can stand this suffering? Men are separated from their wives and children and only when they take us out to eat can they see them. When a man wants to ask his wife something, or when a father wants to see his child, they don't let him. Children get sick, they are taken to a hospital, and it often happens that they never come back.

Because today is a holiday, the Fourth of July, they didn't send anyone back. But Tuesday, the fifth, they begin again to lead us to the "slaughter," that is, to the boat. And God knows how many Jewish lives this will cost, because more than one mind dwells on the thought of jumping into the water when they take him to the boat.

All our hope is that you, Mr. Editor, will not refuse us, and print our letter which is signed by many immigrants. The women have not signed, because they don't let us get to them.

This letter is written by one of the immigrants, a student from Petersburg University, at Castle Garden, July 4, 1909, on the eve of the fast day of *Shivah Asar B'Tamuz* [the seventeenth day of the month of *Tamuz*, when Jews fast in memory of Nebuchadnezzar's siege and destruction of Jerusalem].

Alexander Rudnev

One hundred immigrants, aged from eight to fifty-eight, had signed this letter (each one had included his age). To stir up public opinion and the Jewish organizations, the letter was printed on page 1 with an appeal for action to help the unfortunates. To affirm the authenticity of the facts in the letter, the *Forward* stated that in the English press it had been announced that during the previous week six hundred detained immigrants had been sent back. And on the day the letter from the one hundred was printed, they were sending back two hundred and seventy people.

The *Forward* had previously printed many protests against the unjust treatment of the immigrants confined on Ellis Island, also against the fact that masses were being sent back, and the *Forward* was not silent on this letter.

1909

Dear Mr. Editor,

I was born in a small town in Russia, and until I was sixteen I studied in *Talmud Torahs* and *yeshivas,* but when I came to America I changed quickly. I was influenced by the progressive newspapers, the literature, I developed spiritually and became a freethinker. I meet with free-thinking, progressive people, I feel comfortable in their company and agree with their convictions.

But the nature of my feelings is remarkable. Listen to me: Every year when the month of *Elul* rolls around, when the time of *Rosh Hashanah* and *Yom Kippur* approaches, my heart grows heavy and sad. A melancholy descends on me, a longing gnaws at my breast. At that time I cannot rest, I wander about through the streets, lost in thought, depressed.

When I go past a synagogue during these days and hear a cantor chanting the melodies of the prayers, I become very gloomy and my depression is so great that I cannot endure it. My memory goes back to my happy childhood years. I see clearly before me the small town, the fields, the little pond and the woods around it. I recall my childhood friends and our sweet childlike faith. My heart is constricted, and I begin to run like a madman till the tears stream from my eyes and then I become calmer.

These emotions and these moods have become stronger over the years and I decided to go to the synagogue. I went not in order to pray to God but to heal and refresh my aching soul with the cantor's sweet melodies, and this had an unusually good effect on me.

Sitting in the synagogue among *landsleit* and listening to the good cantor, I forgot my unhappy weekday life, the dirty shop, my boss, the bloodsucker, and my pale, sick wife and my children. All of my America with its hurry-up life was forgotten.

I am a member of a Progressive Society, and since I am known there as an outspoken freethinker, they began to criticize me for going to the synagogue. The members do not want to hear of my personal emotions and they won't understand that there are people whose natures are such that memories of their childhood are sometimes stronger than their convictions.

And where can one hide on *Yom Kippur*? There are many of us, like me. They don't go to work, so it would be good if there could be a meeting hall where they could gather to hear a concert, a lecture, or something else.

What is your opinion of this? Awaiting your answer, I remain,

Your reader,
S.R.

ANSWER:

No one can tell another what to do with himself on *Yom Kippur*. If one is drawn to the synagogue, that is his choice. Naturally, a genuinely sincere freethinker is not drawn to the synagogue. The writer of this letter is full of memories of his childhood days at home, and therefore the cantor's melodies influence him so strongly. Who among us isn't moved by a religious melody remembered from his youth? This, however, has no bearing on loyalty to one's convictions. On *Yom Kippur*, a freethinker can spend his time in a library or with friends. On this day he should not flaunt himself in the eyes of the religious people. There is no sense in arousing their feelings. Every man has a right to live according to his beliefs. The pious man has as much right to his religion as the freethinker to his atheism. To parade one's acts that insult the religious feeling of the pious, especially on *Yom Kippur*, the day they hold most holy, is simply inhuman.

1909

Dear Editor,

Please print my letter and give me an answer. You might possibly save my life with it. I have no peace, neither day nor night, and I am afraid I will go mad because of my dreams.

I came to America three years ago from a small town in Lithuania, and I was twenty years old at that time. Besides me, my parents had five more unmarried daughters. My father was a Hebrew teacher. We used to help out by plucking chickens, making cigarettes, washing clothes for people, and we lived in poverty. The house was like a Gehenna. There was always yelling, cursing, and even beating of each other. It was bitter for me till a cousin of mine took pity on me. He sent a steamship ticket and money. He wrote that I should come to America and he would marry me.

I didn't know him, because he was a little boy when he left our town, but my delight knew no bounds. When I came to him, I found he was a sick man, and a few weeks later he died.

Then I began to work on ladies' waists. The "pleasant" life of a girl in the dreary shop must certainly be familiar to you. I toiled, and like all shopgirls, I hoped and waited for deliverance through a good match.

Landsleit and matchmakers were busy. I met plenty of prospective bridegrooms, but though I was attractive and well built, no one grabbed me. Thus a year passed. Then I met a woman who told me she was a matchmaker and had many suitors "in stock." I spilled out all my heartaches to her. First she talked me out of marrying a work-worn operator with whom I would have to live in poverty, then she told me that pretty girls could wallow in pleasure if they made the right friends. She made such a connection for me. But I had not imagined what that meant.

What I lived through afterwards is impossible for me to describe. The woman handed me over to bandits, and when I wanted to run away from them they locked me in a room without windows and beat me savagely.

Time passed and I got used to the horrible life. Later I even had an opportunity to escape, because they used to send me out on the streets, but life had become meaningless for me anyway, and nothing mattered any more. I lived this way for six months, degraded and dejected, until I got sick and they drove me out of that house.

I appealed for admission into several hospitals, but they didn't want to take me in. I had no money, because the rogues had taken everything from me. I tried to appeal to *landsleit* for help, but since they already knew all about me, they chased me away. I had decided to throw myself into the river, but wandering around on the streets, I met a richly dressed man who was quite drunk. I took over six hundred dollars from him and spent the money on doctors, who cured me.

Then I got a job as a maid for fine people who knew nothing about my past, and I have been working for them for quite a while. I am devoted and diligent, they like me, and everything is fine.

A short time ago the woman of the house died, but I continued to work there. In time, her husband proposed that I marry him. The children, who are not yet grown up, also want me to be their "mother." I know it would be good for them and for me to remain there. The man is honest and good; but my heart won't allow me to deceive him and conceal my past. What shall I do now?

Miserable

ANSWER:
Such letters from victims of "white slavery" come to our attention quite often, but we do not publish them. We are disgusted by this plague on society, and dislike bringing it to the attention of our readers. But as we read this letter we felt we dare not discard it, because it can serve as a warning for other girls. They must, in

their dreary lives, attempt to withstand these temptations and guard themselves from going astray.

This letter writer, who comes to us with her bitter and earnest tears, asking advice, has sufficient reason to fear that if the man finds out about her past he will send her away. But it is hard to conceal something that many people know. Such a thing cannot be kept secret forever. When the man finds out about it from someone else, he would feel that she had betrayed him and it would be worse.

Therefore, "Honesty is the best policy." She should tell him the truth, and whatever will be, will be.

1910

Worthy Editor,

I have been here in America several years, with my father and three sisters. We left Mother and two younger sisters back home. We kept sending money to them and hoped for the time when Mother and our two sisters could come here too.

Finally they started out. Suddenly we got a letter from Mother telling us that on the way one of our sisters, eighteen years of age, was detained because she had trachoma in her eyes, and they all turned back home.

Now we want to write our mother that she should leave our sister at home for a time and come here with our other sister. Though we all feel guilty at the thought of leaving our sister alone, we question whether it is right for the whole family to suffer because of one.

We beg you to give your advice on how to act. Five people wait impatiently for your answer.

Respectfully,
H.G.
Detroit, Michigan

ANSWER:

If the eighteen-year-old girl has to remain alone, it is not fair to leave her. If, however, she can stay there with family or friends, there is nothing to worry about. The point is that she must see to it that her eyes are cured as soon as possible, so that she can be brought to America more quickly, and the family can be together.

1910

Worthy Editor,

When we came to America ten years ago we struggled and went through a lot. My husband didn't have a trade and couldn't find any kind of job. We suffered from hunger and cold. Our two little children stretched their bony little hands out to us, begging for food, and I had none to give them. I shudder when I think of those terrible times.

At that time we lived in a basement, and because we owed the landlord six dollars for rent, he put us out on the street. I huddled with the two children near our few belongings and my husband ran to his *landsleit* to beg their help.

The neighbors and passers-by threw a few cents into a plate that was placed on our broken-down table; looking at us, seeing the tragic picture, everyone was moved. But the clang of the coins falling into the plate tore at my heart and I wept bitter tears. I want to mention here that I came from a respectable family and my parents had given me a dowry of six hundred rubles.

Toward evening my husband came back, disheartened and defeated, and told me that his *landsleit* were poverty-stricken too, and he couldn't get more than two dollars from them.

Just then a well-dressed young woman came by, stopped to talk to us and told us to come home with her and she would give us money for the rent. My husband went with her and soon came back overjoyed. He told me the woman had given him twenty-five dollars and asked us to come to her home for supper.

When I came into the house with my children, I immediately felt at home, because the woman, the good angel, couldn't do enough for us. After supper she went out shopping for clothing for the children, whom she constantly hugged and kissed. Her husband was no less fine and goodhearted to us. He promised to find a job for my husband and he did.

We rented rooms and started life anew. In time my husband bought a business and the two good people helped us a great deal. We became very friendly with them and not a day passed that we didn't see each other. For the last four years we have been living in the same house where they live.

I am now the mother of five children and we live quite happily. But lately something happened that upset us a great deal. The couple who helped us so much have no children. They are well off, they love each other, but they long for a child. And they are very attached to our children.

Recently, with tears in her eyes, the woman poured out her heart to me and complained that she enjoyed nothing and was very lonely. When I tried to comfort her, she said that I could help her. I told her I would gladly do anything in the world for her. Then she told me she wanted me to give her my youngest child, who is almost two years old. Her words shocked me and I told her I had to talk it over with my husband.

Well, my husband is ready to give her the child, but I can't do it. I would give her my life, but how can a mother give away her own child? She cries and begs for the child, whom she loves very much. Her husband pleads with her to put it out of her mind, but it doesn't help. I am afraid that it might end in a tragedy.

I wait in despair for your advice.

With thanks,
A Perplexed Mother

ANSWER:

In the answer this couple, who helped the family in their dire need, are praised highly for their charitable deeds. But it is explained to the childless woman that she dare not and must not demand of these people, who are so grateful to her, that they give away one of their five children. Also, the father of the children is told that he has no right to try to convince his wife to give their child to the benefactress.

1910

Worthy Editor,

My husband, —— [here the name was given], deserted me and our three small children, leaving us in desperate need. I was left without a bit of bread for the children, with debts in the grocery store and the butcher's, and last month's rent unpaid.

I am not complaining so much about his abandoning me as about the grief and suffering of our little children, who beg for food, which I cannot give them. I am young and healthy, I am able and willing to work in order to support my children, but unfortunately I am tied down because my baby is only six months old. I looked for an institution which would take care of my baby, but my friends advise against it.

The local Jewish Welfare Agencies are allowing me and my children to die of hunger, and this is because my "faithful" husband brought me over from Canada just four months ago and therefore I do not yet deserve to eat their bread.

It breaks my heart but I have come to the conclusion that in order to save my innocent children from hunger and cold I have to give them away.

I will sell my beautiful children to people who will give them a home. I will sell them, not for money, but for bread, for a secure home where they will have enough food and warm clothing for the winter.

I, the unhappy young mother, am willing to sign a contract, with my heart's blood, stating that the children belong to the good people who will treat them tenderly. Those who are willing and able to give my children a good home can apply to me.

Respectfully,
Mrs. P.*
Chicago

ANSWER:

What kind of society are we living in that forces a mother to such desperate straits that there is no other way out than to sell her three children for a piece of bread? Isn't this enough to kindle a hellish fire of hatred in every human heart for such a system?

The first to be damned is the heartless father, but who knows what's wrong with him? Perhaps he, too, is unhappy. We hope, though, that this letter will reach him and he will return to aid them.

We also ask our friends and readers to take an interest in this unfortunate woman and to help her so that she herself can be a mother to her children.

1910

Dear Editor,

Since I do not want my conscience to bother me, I ask you to decide whether a married woman has the right to go to school two evenings a week. My husband thinks I have no right to do this.

I admit that I cannot be satisfied to be just a wife and mother. I am still young and I want to learn and enjoy life. My children and my house are not neglected, but I go to evening high school twice a week. My husband is not pleased and when I come home at night and ring the bell, he lets me stand outside a long time intentionally, and doesn't hurry to open the door.

* The full name and address here given.

Now he has announced a new decision. Because I send out the laundry to be done, it seems to him that I have too much time for myself, even enough to go to school. So from now on he will count out every penny for anything I have to buy for the house, so I will not be able to send out the laundry any more. And when I have to do the work myself there won't be any time left for such "foolishness" as going to school. I told him that I'm willing to do my own washing but that I would still be able to find time for study.

When I am alone with my thoughts, I feel I may not be right. Perhaps I should not go to school. I want to say that my husband is an intelligent man and he wanted to marry a woman who was educated. The fact that he is intelligent makes me more annoyed with him. He is in favor of the emancipation of women, yet in real life he acts contrary to his beliefs.

Awaiting your opinion on this, I remain,

Your reader,
The Discontented Wife

ANSWER:

Since this man is intelligent and an adherent of the women's emancipation movement, he is scolded severely in the answer for wanting to keep his wife so enslaved. Also the opinion is expressed that the wife absolutely has the right to go to school two evenings a week.

1910

Dear Editor,

This is the voice of thirty-seven miserable men who are buried but not covered over by earth, tied down but not in chains, silent but not mute, whose hearts beat like humans, yet are not like other human beings.

When we look at our striped clothes, at our dirty narrow

cots, at our fellow companions in the cells, the beaten, lowest members of society, who long ago lost their human dignity, the blood freezes in our veins. We feel degraded and miserable here. And why are we confined here? For the horrible crime of being poor, not being able to satisfy the mad whims of our wives. That's why we pine away here, stamped with the name "convict." That's why we are despised, robbed of our freedom, and treated like dogs.

We ask you, worthy Editor, to publish our letter so your readers, especially the women, will know how we live here. This letter is written not with ink but with our hearts' blood. We are coughing from the polluted air that we breathe in the cells. Our bones ache from lying on the hard cots and we get stomach-aches from the food they give us.

The non-support "plague" is the worst plague of all. For the merest nonsense, a man is caught and committed to the work-house. He doesn't even get a chance to defend himself. Even during the worst times of the Russian reaction people didn't suffer as the men suffer here in America because of their wives. For a Jewish wife it's as easy here to condemn her husband to imprisonment as it is for her to try on a pair of gloves. In all the world there isn't such legal injustice as here in the alimony courts.

What do they think, these women! If they believe that the imprisoned husbands, after the six months, will become purified and come out good, sweet and loving, they're making a big mistake.

The worst offense is committed by the Jewish charity organizations. They sympathize with the wife when her husband is in jail. They forget, however, that they "manufacture" the grass widows and living orphans when they help the woman. As soon as the wife tastes an easy and a free dollar, as soon as she discovers that the "charities" won't let her starve, she doesn't care that her husband is condemned. She lives a gay life, enjoys herself, and doesn't think of her husband.

Therefore it is your duty as editor of the *Forward*, the newspaper that is read mainly by the working class, the class that furnishes more than all others the candidates for the workhouse and for grass widowhood, to warn all the Jewish women not to take such revenge on their husbands. They do more harm to themselves than to their men. They drive away their husbands for life that way, and make themselves and their children miserable. The women must learn that sending their husbands to prison is a poor method of improving them. It is a double-edged sword that slashes one side as deeply as the other.

Finally, I appeal to all the women whose husbands are imprisoned for non-support in the workhouse on Blackwell's Island Prison, and I write to them as follows: Their husbands have sworn here that if they, the women, do not have them released in time for *Pesach*, they will never again return and the women will remain grass widows forever.

We ask you to publish this letter immediately.

> Respectfully,
> [The letter is signed by thirty-seven men]

ANSWER:

The answer emphasizes the fact that the great number of men who avoid supporting their wives and children commit a serious crime. True, sending them to prison doesn't have the desired effect, but they deserve to be punished for not doing their duty. It certainly doesn't pay for the women to have their husbands arrested for the little bit of "charity" they get. It's ridiculous to think they can live a gay life on that pittance.

It is also remarked that among these thirty-seven men there must also be some who weren't in a position to support their families, but it's nothing new to find innocent men suffering along with the guilty.

Finally, the women are advised to see to it that their husbands are released for *Pesach*.

1910

Dear Editor,

Just as there is agitation about the cloakmakers' strike everywhere, so is it also discussed in our society of *landsleit*. A committee from the cloakmakers was sent to one of our meetings to ask for support for the strike, but our treasury was closed for six months by a resolution of the members, and no expenditures may be voted. Knowing that time is valuable to the cloakmakers, we began a debate about it after we sent the committee away. As president of the society, I had to speak in the interests of the group, though I am a friend of the workers.

A motion was made to tax the brothers at the next meeting to raise money for the strikers. But the motion was defeated by the members with the argument that each one could, of his own free will, make his own contribution to the strike.

We did not come to any conclusion, and the meeting was adjourned. Knowing the condition of the strikers, I decided not to wait for a second meeting and I brought into the *Forward* office a contribution of five dollars for the striking cloakmakers in the name of our organization. I plan, also, that in the future, whenever it is urgent to support any cause during the time our treasury is closed, I will donate up to twenty-five dollars, without consulting the membership. I believe I can do this, as president, because it is in the interest of the organization.

I know that when I bring it up at the next meeting there will be some who oppose this and will say I have no right to do it, so I ask for your opinion. I would like to hear from you whether I had the right to act on my own and give aid to the strikers.

Thank you,
A Constant Reader

ANSWER:

We certainly want a great deal of money to come in for the strikers. But what's true is true: a president does not have the right to give contributions or to make any disbursements without the agreement of the membership.

1910

Dear Editor,

I am an operator on ladies' waists for the past four years and I earn good wages. I work steady but haven't saved money, because I have a sick wife. I had to put her in the hospital where she lay for four weeks, and then I had to bring her home.

Just after I brought her home, the General Strike began and I could see that I was in trouble. I had to go to the union to beg them not to let me down in my situation. I just asked for some money to have a little soup for my sick wife, but they answered that there wasn't any money. I struggled along with my wife for four weeks, and when I saw that I might lose her I had to go back to work at the shop where we were striking. Now my conscience bothers me because I am a scab.

I am working now, I bring home fifteen, sometimes sixteen dollars a week. But I am not happy, because I was a scab and left the union. I want to state here that I was always a good union man.

Dear Editor, how can I now go back in the union and salve my conscience? I am ready to swear that I will remain a loyal union man forever.

Your reader,
F.H.

ANSWER:

Neither the operator nor the union is guilty. During the strike, thousands upon thousands of workers complained that they were in need, but at the beginning of the strike there really was no money.

It is now the duty of the union to investigate the case, and if it is shown that circumstances were as the operator describes, they will certainly forgive him and he can again become a good union man.

1911

Worthy Editor,

Please do me a service and print my letter, because in a few days I will no longer be among the living. I have picked the twenty-sixth of January to make an end to my life, because that is my birthday. On that day I was born and on that day I will die. I am not writing this letter to ask for advice, because there is nothing that can help me any more. I write only to ask forgiveness for what I am going to do in the twenty-fifth year of my life.

I ask my friends to see to it that my body is cremated. I will leave a letter to those who can carry this out. The reason I came to this decision is that I have already been sick for a few years. But it was never as bad as it is now.

What ails me? I am haggard, anemic, and my face is ashen. I am weak and suffer from headaches; my eyes close as soon as night falls. There is a terrible odor from my mouth and I am ashamed to talk to anyone. My teeth are blackened and decayed; my nose is constantly clogged and I must always keep my mouth open to breathe. I have no way of earning a living. I am a garment worker but I have no strength to work.

I am lonely here in the country where I have been for five years and I believe that's long enough, that it's time I should free myself from my troubles. My "freedom" is already standing on the table in my bedroom.

I beg forgiveness from my friends. Good-by.

Respectfully,
The Unfortunate One from Stanton Street, New York

ANSWER:

We print this letter with the hope that perhaps some readers will recognize the writer and manage to rescue him. Possibly he is only influenced by melancholia and his condition is actually not as tragic as he describes it. It may be that if he consulted a good doctor he could still get well.

1911

Dear Editor,

I am writing to you here about a serious matter because I need your advice.

My husband and I were married for nineteen years and we have two sons, seventeen and fifteen years old. We were divorced three months ago because we hadn't been getting along.

But now we have reconsidered and realize we made a grave mistake, and we want to correct it. We wanted to remarry but we have difficulties. My husband is a *kohen*, and no rabbi will perform a religious ceremony for us. The rabbis we went to explained that it is against the Jewish law for a *kohen* to marry a divorced woman.

Therefore I ask you for advice, because we don't know what to do now. We aren't religious fanatics, but we want to handle this so that it will be proper in people's eyes.

We await your answer and will accept your advice.

Thank you in advance,
Mrs. R.D.K.

ANSWER:

Handling this problem in a way that would be proper and suit everyone is impossible. If they decide to live together, without being married by a rabbi, it would be considered proper by free-thinkers but not by religious people. If they obey the Jewish law and remain separate, it would be in accord with the Orthodox tradition. However, they don't have to ask anyone's advice, but should act according to their own convictions.

1911

Dear Editor,

I plead with you to open your illustrious newspaper and take in my "Bintel Brief" in which I write about my great suffering.

A long gloomy year, three hundred and sixty-five days, have gone by since I left my home and am alone on the lonely road of life. Oh, my poor dear parents, how saddened they were at my leaving. The leave-taking, their seeing me on my way, was like a silent funeral.

There was no shaking of the alms box, there was no grave digging and no sawing of boards, but I, myself, put on the white shirt that was wet with my mother's tears, took my pillow, and climbed into the wagon. Accompanying me was a quiet choked wail from my parents and friends.

The wheels of the wagon rolled farther and farther away. My mother and father wept for their son, then turned with heavy hearts to the empty house. They did not sit *shive* even though they had lost a child.

I came to America and became a painter. My great love for Hebrew, for Russian, all of my other knowledge was smeared with paint. During the year that I have been here I have had some good periods, but I am not happy, because I have no interest in anything. My homesickness and loneliness darken my life.

Ah, home, my beloved home. My heart is heavy for my parents whom I left behind. I want to run back, but I am powerless. I am a coward, because I know that I have to serve under *"Fonie"* [the Czar] for three years. I am lonely in my homesickness and I beg you to be my counsel as to how to act.

Respectfully,
V.A.

ANSWER:
The answer states that almost all immigrants yearn deeply for dear ones and home at first. They are compared with plants that are transplanted to new ground. At first it seems that they are withering, but in time most of them revive and take root in the new earth.

The advice to this young man is that he must not consider going home, but try to take root here. He should try to overcome all these emotions and strive to make something of himself so that in time he will be able to bring his parents here.

Most of the immigrants were young boys or girls whose parents had sent them on to America. They were to earn enough money to send for their parents later on. Naturally these young boys and girls were very lonesome for their mothers and their homes, and on Saturday afternoon the Thalia Theater in New York was filled with shopgirls who had a good cry listening to Lucy German sing "Eibega Mama [Eternal Mother]."

1911

Dear Editor,

I am a newsboy, fourteen years old, and I sell the *Forverts* in the streets till late into the night. I come to you to ask your advice.

I was born in Russia and was twelve years old when I came

to America with my dear mother. My sister, who was in the country before us, brought us over.

My sister worked and supported us. She didn't allow me to go to work but sent me to school. I went to school for two years and didn't miss a day, but then came the terrible fire at the Triangle shop, where she worked, and I lost my dear sister. My mother and I suffer terribly from the misfortune. I had to help my mother and after school hours I go out and sell newspapers.

I have to go to school three more years, and after that I want to go to college. But my mother doesn't want me to go to school because she thinks I should go to work. I tell her I will work days and study at night but she won't hear of it.

Since I read the *Forverts* to my mother every night and read your answers in the "Bintel Brief," I beg you to answer me and say a few words to her.

Your Reader,
The Newsboy

ANSWER:
The answer to this letter is directed to the boy's mother, whose daughter was one of the shopworkers who perished in the Triangle fire. The unfortunate woman is comforted in the answer, and she is told that she must not hinder her son's nighttime studies but must help him reach his goal. And an appeal is made to good people who are in a position to do something for the boy to come forward and help him further his education.

The Triangle fire was a disaster. My mother along with other East Side mothers hung a piece of black crepe out of the window on the day of the funeral. All the girls were buried in the Workman's Circle Cemetery and the cortege was followed by some hundred thousand workers.

1912

Dear Editor,

Twenty-two years ago I came to America with my wife and our four little children. We lived in Chicago nineteen years, and we have been in New York for three. I am not skilled in a trade, but I am a businessman, and all these years I've struggled because I never made a living. I know English, I am not lazy, I've tried everything and never succeeded.

When the children were young I had to appeal for aid to my wealthy family in Warsaw, and they helped me many times. Later, as the children grew up and began to earn money, it was easier, but I, with all my ability as a businessman, couldn't get myself settled in this country. In the city of Warsaw, where I lived before emigrating to America, there were times when things weren't too bad. In America, however, it always went badly and I haven't been able to adjust to the country.

Now, when my children are all married and in good positions, I got an idea that it might be good for me and my wife to go back to Warsaw. It is very hard to part with the children, but to live in poverty is also bad. It seems strange to me that I must go away from the free America in order to better my condition. But the chances for me are still better there. I ask your advice, and I thank you in advance.

Respectfully,
The Unlucky One

ANSWER:
The advice to this letter writer is not to go back to Warsaw, because after so many years in this country, he would feel like a stranger there. He must understand he is no longer the same man he was twenty-two years ago, and the city of Warsaw is also not the same as it was in the past.

1912

Worthy Editor,

I am a twenty-eight-year-old woman, married for six years, and my only trouble is that I have no children. My husband makes a good living and my friends envy me. But they don't know my heartaches. My husband eats my heart out with a few words, like rust eats iron. He keeps saying it's "nearer than farther" to the ten-year limit when, according to Jewish law, I will have to give him a divorce if I don't have a baby by that time.

I can't find words to express to you how I suffer from these remarks. He's drawing my blood drop by drop and I'm sinking from day to day.

A short time ago I was quite sick and he spent a lot of money to cure me. When I got well my husband said to me, "You'll have to earn your own living, so I want you to be healthy."

Dear Editor, I am all alone here, and I ask you to advise me what to do. Can my husband get a divorce after the ten years through the court too? I know he can get it through a rabbi. I am ready to leave him now, if he is unhappy with me. How shall I act?

Respectfully yours,
Suffering and Lonely

ANSWER:

The answer is that the statutes of the country do not accept the Jewish law, and the writer's husband cannot get a legal divorce. In addition the man is scolded for his inhuman behavior toward his wife. He is told that a civilized man doesn't cast out his faithful wife just because she has no children. The wife is also consoled and given the hope that before the ten years are up she might become a mother.

1913

Worthy Mr. Editor,

I am a young woman, married eight years to a man who came from Russia, and we have four beautiful children. My husband's parents were killed in a pogrom and he alone barely escaped with his life. Later he was forced to leave Russia and he came to America.

Since the world-famed case of Mendel Beilis began in Russia, my husband doesn't miss reading anything that is written about it. And every time he finishes reading something in the newspaper about the bloodthirsty trial he gets so upset, so nervous, that he sometimes shows signs of madness. More than once I've been afraid to stay alone in the house with him.

At first it was bearable, but lately the news about the trial affected his nerves so much that he took it into his head that he must go back to Russia to take revenge on Beilis' persecutors. He had already packed his bags, but when he began to take leave of the children, to say good-by, they began to cry so bitterly that he remained at home. But he keeps on saying that he must go to Russia to take revenge on those who falsely accused Beilis of the ritual murder and on the pogromists who killed his own parents.

A few days ago he went to a lawyer and signed over to me and the children the few hundred dollars he has in the bank. He told me he did this so that, in case something happened to him in Russia, the children and I would at least have the few dollars.

Therefore, dear Editor, I need your advice. Maybe your answer will calm him a little, and he will put these ideas out of his head.

I thank you in advance,
Mary

ANSWER:

Thousands of Jews come to America with their pogrom wounds
that still bleed and can never be completely healed. And is it any
wonder that this writer's husband has shattered nerves? The murderers there killed his parents, almost brought about his death,
and now the dreadful Beilis trial has reopened his old wounds.

Russia is full of such people, Jews and non-Jews, who feel
the same hatred as he for the "Black Hundreds," and if it were
possible to take revenge on the guilty ones they wouldn't wait for
him to come all the way from America. But time will pay them
what's due them. This man must calm himself, he must have
pity on his wife and children and stop thinking of leaving them.
The most important point is, however, that the wife must take
him to a good psychiatrist.

*Several letters in the Bintel Brief refer to the Mendel Beilis
case in Russia in 1911. In March 1911 a Russian boy was found
murdered in Kiev. The anti-Semitic organizations began a cam-
paign charging that the crime, having been committed on the eve
of Passover, must be treated as nothing less than ritual murder.
The accusation fell upon Mendel Beilis, a Jew, the manager of a
local brick factory, and by 1913 the case seethed throughout
the world. Seventy-four distinguished American Christian clergymen and the Catholic cardinal in Vienna denounced the folly
as a vicious fable to the Czar. But, where anti-Semitism is concerned, all logic is irrelevant, including the fact that this charge
was first brought against the Christians and had sent hundreds of
them into the Roman arena to face gladiators and beasts.
(Through the centuries the Freemasons were also accused of
ritual murder, once on the floor of the American Congress by
Thaddeus Stevens, the fanatical enemy of the South.) The in-
nocence of Beilis had no weight at all. But this time world
opinion was very strong. The religious, political and intellectual
leaders of every civilized country sent protests. Beilis was acquitted
and, against the advice of his lawyers, went back to his little
home in the country where, to his surprise, he was greeted with*

sympathy and congratulations by his Gentile fellow workers. Shortly afterward, he left to live in Palestine and eventually the United States where he died. The belief, however, remained in spite of his acquittal, that the brutal act represented a ritual murder. Eventually, a notorious woman criminal confessed that it was she and her gang who had murdered the boy as a suspected stool pigeon.

1913

Dear Editor,

I come from Europe, where I was brought up by a father who was a *Talmud* scholar and a cantor. I took after my father both in learning and voice, and when I became a *Bar Mitzvah* my leading the congregation in prayer impressed everyone. My name became known in many cities and people came to hear me conduct the services.

When I turned eighteen a respected man from a town near Kovne took me as a son-in-law, gave me four hundred rubles and five years of room and board. I married his pretty sixteen-year-old daughter, moved into my father-in-law's house, ate, drank and devoted myself to the study of *Torah*. Once in a while, on a special Sabbath or a holiday, I led the prayers in *shul*, but I took no money for that.

After the five years I was left with a pretty young wife, two children and my dowry money. My father-in-law then established for me, or I should say for my wife, a small grocery and told me, "You will continue to study *Torah* and your wife will make a living for you." But my wife wasn't very good at business and the money went fast. Meanwhile, my father-in-law died, my mother-in-law went to her son in Kovne, and we were left alone.

I began to talk to my wife about going to America and after long deliberation we left home. When we came to this country, our *landsleit* helped us a little to get settled and when the High

Holy Days came, I earned a hundred and eighty dollars as a cantor leading the *Musaph* prayers. I began to make a living as a cantor, and people hired me for weddings, funerals and other affairs.

As time went on my horizons broadened. I read all kinds of books, I accumulated worldly knowledge and I began to look at life quite differently.

In short, I can't reconcile myself to continue making a living as a cantor, because I am no longer religious. I can't act against my conscience, and the right thing to do is to give up my present livelihood. I want to learn a trade now, perhaps become a peddler or find another means of earning a living that has nothing to do with religion.

My wife, who held onto her old beliefs and is still fanatical, doesn't even want to hear of my plans. She argues that serving as a cantor is honorable. It is also questionable whether I can earn enough to support a family from working in a shop or from peddling.

Now there are arguments about this between me, my wife and our close friends, and we all decided to place the question in your hands. I want to hear what you have to say about it.

Your reader,
The Progressive Cantor

ANSWER:
Freethinkers as well as religious people will answer this question in the same way. Even the rabbi will say that, according to Jewish law, only a pious Jew may be a cantor. His wife and his religious friends who are trying to convince him to remain a cantor are really committing the worst sin according to their beliefs.

For a non-believer to be a cantor for an Orthodox congregation is without a doubt a shameful hypocrisy.

1913

Worthy Mr. Editor,

I am a man who has already lived half my years and I can say that I have never had any peace.

I was born in Russia of poor parents and when quite young I went to Vilna to study at the Romailes *yeshiva*. Later I studied at a *yeshiva* in Kovne. I "ate days" at other people's tables and often went hungry because there were many times when I had only three "days" a week.

When I was eighteen I came home to my parents. Because I had been registered in error as a few years older, I was due to be drafted for military service. So it was decided that I go to America. I went through a lot until I finally saw the "Golden Land," and here during the first years I suffered a great deal. I worked at many jobs, beginning with peddling, till I became an operator. I also had enough to put up with in the shop from the boss, the foreman and even certain workers. But no matter how hard I worked, I always used my free time to continue learning.

In time I married a girl who was as lonely as I, and we were happy, even though I made a meager living. When our big-mouth, the "Workers' Liberator," Teddy Roosevelt, was elected for his second term, it got so bad that I couldn't find a job. We had five children by then and no money coming in. I became a janitor, and for the work I was given two dark little rooms (on Stanton Street) where the sun was ashamed to shine.

Once, when I went out to look for work, I accidentally met a friend with whom I had studied years ago in Vilna. I was thin as a rail, but he was well fed, had a big belly and was well dressed. I asked him what he does for a living, but he didn't answer, only invited me to his home. There he told me that if I wanted to I could be as well off as he. In short, he told me he was a missionary and got a hundred seventy-five dollars a month, not counting gifts.

I was in a tight spot and I let him talk me into it. I also became a traitor to my people and devoted myself to preaching Christian doctrine to Jews. How much I now regret that I agreed to it. I know that such a degraded person does not deserve sympathy and cannot be forgiven.

When my wife, who was religious, found out that I had become a missionary, she didn't want to know me any longer. I was sent to do my work in N—— State and I didn't hear from my wife and children. From aggravation I got sick, became paralyzed and lay in the hospital for a time. Lying there, lonely and sick, I had enough time to think about my "occupation," about the gang of missionaries and about the fact that I had paid dearly for the stupid step which I now regretted.

I have left the hospital and the doctor says I will recover fully so I decided to go back to work in the shop again.

I cannot demand sympathy from my wife, because I do not deserve it, but I hope you will print my letter. Maybe my wife will read it and perhaps at least let me know where she is and how my children are, because I would like to help them out. I also hope that my letter will serve as a warning to others to beware of making the terrible mistake I made.

> With respect,
> Unhappy

ANSWER:
This is the reward for treachery, for preaching something one does not himself believe in. If the writer of this letter is now sincere and has really repented, his wife should forgive him and come back to him with the children. She must remember that even God himself receives a penitent with open arms.

The Hebrew-Christian evangelists are a big nuisance to the Jewish communities of the South. They have their big advertisements in the paper; "Come hear the Jew who has seen the light and accepted Jesus." Their audiences are composed of Southern Baptists and Methodists but only once in a great while is there a

Jew among them. I have spoken to most of these Hebrew-Christian evangelists in the South, notably Jacob Garterhaus and Hyman Glass, and they admit that they make very little headway among the Jews. But they make a good living preaching to the Gentiles, who love to see a Jew on the platform who has been converted to Christianity.

1914

Worthy Mr. Editor,

I, an old woman of seventy, write you this letter with my heart's blood, because I am distressed.

In Galicia, I was a respected housewife and my husband was a well-known businessman. God blessed us with three daughters and three sons and we raised them properly. When they grew up, one by one they left home, like birds leaving their nest. Our daughters got married, and later left for America with their husbands. Our oldest son also married but a month after his wedding a misfortune befell us—he went swimming and was drowned.

This tragedy had such a bad effect on my husband that he neglected his business, began to ail, and died. The two younger sons both went to America after that, and I was left alone. I longed for the children and wrote to them that I wanted to come to America, to be with them and the grandchildren. But from the first they wrote me that America was not for me, that they do not keep *kosher* and that I would be better off staying at home.

But I didn't let them convince me, and I went to America. All of my children came to meet me at the boat, and I will never forget that moment when they and my grandchildren hugged me and kissed me. Is there any greater happiness for a mother?

But now a new trouble has fallen on me. A few weeks ago when Austria declared war and we heard that Russia was fighting against Austria, my two sons, who are ardent patriots of Kaiser Franz Josef, announced that they were sailing home to help him in the war. When I heard this, I began to cry and begged them not to rush into the fire because they would be shortening my life. But so far they have not given up the idea of going to fight for the Kaiser.

Worthy Editor, I hope you will voice your opinion on this serious matter. Maybe you can have influence on them to give up the idea of leaving this country and their old mother, and going to war.

Your reader,
The Suffering Mother

ANSWER:
In the answer it says that the woman's two sons should thank God that they are in America, where they are free and can't be forced to shed their blood for the Austrian Kaiser.

1914

Worthy Editor,

I am a girl twenty-two years of age, but I've already undergone a great deal in my life. When I was born I already had no father. He died four months before my birth. And when I was three weeks old my mother died too. Grandmother, my mother's mother, took me in and soon gave me away to a poor tailor's wife to suckle me.

I was brought up by the tailor and his wife, and got so used to them that I called them Mother and Father. When I grew up I learned from the tailor how to do hand sewing and machine sewing too.

When I was sixteen my grandmother died and left me her small dilapidated house. The rabbi of the town sold it for me for three hundred rubles and gave me the money.

In time one of the tailor's apprentices fell in love with me, and I didn't reject his love. He was a fine, honest, quiet young man and a good earner. He had a golden character and we became as one body and soul. When I turned seventeen my bridegroom came to me with a plan, that we should go to America, and I agreed.

It was hard for me to take leave of the tailor's good family, who had kept me as their own child, and oceans of tears were shed when we parted.

When we came to America my bridegroom immediately started to work and he supported me. He was faithful and devoted. I'll give you an example of his loyalty: once, during the summer in the terrible heat, I slept on the roof. But it started to rain in the middle of the night and I was soaked through to the bone. I got very sick and had to be taken to the hospital. I was so sick that the doctor said I could be saved only by a blood transfusion. My bridegroom said immediately that he was ready to give me his blood, and so, thanks to him, I recovered.

In time I went to work at the "famous" Triangle shop. Later my bridegroom also got a job there. Even at work he wanted to be with me. My bridegroom told me then, "We will both work hard for a while and then we'll get married. We will save every cent so we'll be able to set up a home and then you'll be a housewife and never go to work in the shop again."

Thus my good bridegroom mused about the golden future. Then there was that terrible fire that took one hundred and forty-seven young blossoming lives. When the fire broke out, the screaming, the yelling, the panic all bewildered me. I saw the angel of death before me and my voice was choked in my throat. Suddenly someone seized me with extraordinary strength and carried me out of the shop.

When I recovered I heard calming voices and saw my bridegroom near me. I was in the street, rescued, and saw my girl friends jumping out of the windows and falling to the ground. I clung to my bridegroom and rescuer, but he soon tore himself away from me. "I must save other girls," he said, and disappeared. I never saw him alive again. The next day I identified him, in the morgue, by his watch, which had my pictured pasted under the cover. I fainted and they could hardly bring me to.

After that I lay in the hospital for five weeks, and came home shattered. This is the fourth year that I am alone and I still see before me the horrible scenes of the fire. I still see the good face of my dear bridegroom, also the black burned face in the morgue. I am weak and nervous, yet there is now a young man who wants to marry me. But I made a vow that I would never get married. Besides that, I'm afraid that I will never be able to love another man. But this young man doesn't want to leave me, and my friends try to persuade me to marry him and say everything will be all right. I don't believe it, because I think everything can be all right for me only in the grave.

I decided to write to you, because I want to hear your opinion.

Respectfully,
A Faithful Reader

ANSWER:
It is senseless for this girl to sacrifice her life in memory of her faithful bridegroom, since this would not bring him back to life. What the earth covers must be forgotten. She has suffered enough in her life already and is advised to take herself in hand and begin her life anew.

1915

Worthy Editor,

My biography is similar to those of so many other Jewish people from Lithuania: to *kheyder* at the age of five, had a good head for learning, was religious, then became an unbeliever and later a Zionist. In time I felt that it was not enough to think only of my own people and my heart beat with love for the downtrodden of all nations. I was also arrested as a revolutionary several times, and after that my parents sent me away to America.

Seventeen years have passed since I parted from my parents, but I still see before me my father in his anxiety and feel my mother's hot tears on my face.

My heart pounded with joy when I saw New York in the distance. It was like coming out of the darkness when I left my town. I came to the Big City where I sensed the freedom and I became a proletarian. I looked up several friends who were with me in the revolutionary movement, but I was very disappointed in them because they had lost their old spirit and their ideals. Now they were only interested in a steady job with good wages, and had no time to bother with the old-time "foolishness."

When I came into the shop and saw the pettiness of the workers I had held in such high esteem, when I saw the envy and enmity between them in the shop, I became terribly dejected. I had overthrown the God of my parents and now saw how petty and paltry my new Gods were.

I left New York with its sweatshops, took a bundle of goods, went West, and was no longer a proletarian. A few years later I married a very pretty girl, and for a short time my wife, whom I loved dearly, was everything to me. I thought I had finally found my peace and happiness. Then came my greatest disappointment.

I was in business and got involved with my wife's brother and a good friend of hers. When a fire broke out in my store, they tightened a noose around my neck. My wife and the two of them gave "evidence" that I had set fire to my store to collect the insurance.

I served two years and nine months in the penitentiary but I swear on the memory of my parents, who are no longer living, that I am innocent. I went into prison with a clearer conscience than those who sentenced me. And when I found out that my wife was among those who plotted my downfall, I lost all interest in life and my heart grew cold as ice and hard as stone.

Sitting in my damp cold cell, I thought of taking bloody revenge on those who caused my imprisonment. In time, however, my desire to get even with them weakened. Meanwhile, my wife had divorced me, and when I got out of prison I considered either throwing myself into the river or becoming a drunkard, to forget. I pushed aside those thoughts and went back to earning a living, but the jingling of the silver brought me no solace and the glitter of gold didn't ease my pain.

Four years have passed since I got out of prison, and do you know where I now find my consolation? In the old *Gemore*. Call me an idiot or whatever you want but the *Talmud* takes me away from all earthly things and makes me forget everything they did to me. When I am absorbed in the *Talmud*, I forget my loneliness and sorrow and my room turns into a palace where I am king.

I am a man in my thirties, and I am thinking of returning now to my remote Lithuanian town, to bury myself in the *Talmud* in a corner of the old *shul*, and there live out my years.

What is your advice?

> With thanks and respect,
> L.D.

ANSWER:

In answer to the writer of this letter it is said the solace and inspiration he now finds in life lies not only in the *Talmud* but mainly in the memories of his youth. Further, it would possibly be good for him to go to his old town. Not that he would find peace there, but he might be re-awakened and feel the urgency to tear himself out of the darkness again, to run back to the free world and start anew.

1915

Worthy Editor,

Not long ago some money came into my hands, money that did not belong to me.

This is the second time that such a thing has happened to me.

The first time it was back in Russia. At that time I found a few hundred rubles and, since I knew the money belonged to the boss for whom I worked, I didn't hesitate, but gave it right back to him. At the time I told him that I felt the money wasn't actually his, because he had squeezed it out of us workers.

Now it has happened to me here in America. A few months ago I got a job in a shop where I worked at piecework and, through an error, they paid me more than was coming to me. When I came home with the pay, I saw I had more money than I had earned. I told some of my friends about the mistake and one of them blurted out: "May you well enjoy the money from the boss." Another one said, however, that I should return the money.

The next morning I returned the overpayment to the boss and some of the workers laughed at me. They were of the opinion that I shouldn't have given back the money. But my principle is to take from the boss only what is due me for my work, according to the rate I agreed on with him.

What is your opinion? Hoping you will answer me and clear up this matter, for other workers, I thank you in advance.

Your reader,
M.H.H.

ANSWER:

That's the way an honest worker acts. And whoever laughs at such action and thinks the money should not have been returned is simply a thief. Workers who fight for their rights condemn stealing. Their entire fight is actually against robbery and theft.

1917

Dear Editor,

Four years ago, because of my activity in the revolutionary movement in Russia, I was forced to leave the country and come to America. I had no trade, because I was brought up in a wealthy home, so I struggled terribly at first. Thanks to my education and my ability to adjust, I am now a manager of a large wholesale firm and earn good wages. In time I fell in love with an intelligent, pretty American girl and married her.

America was my new home, and my wife and I tried to live in a way that would be most interesting and pleasant. From time to time, however, I had the desire to visit Russia to see what was going on there. But in America one is always busy and there is no time to be sentimental so I never went.

But now everything is changed. The Russian freedom movement, in which I took part, has conquered Czarism. The ideal for which I fought has become a reality, and my heart draws me there more than ever now. I began to talk about it to my wife, but her answer is that she hasn't the least desire to go to Russia. My revolutionary fire has cooled down here in the practical America, but it is not altogether extinguished, and I'm ready to go home now.

The latest events in Russia do not let me rest, and my mind is not on my job. But my wife and her parents tell me it would be foolish to leave such a good job and ruin everything. My wife doesn't want to go, and she holds me back. I can't leave my wife, whom I love very much, but it's hard to turn my back on my beloved homeland. I don't know how to act and I beg you to advise me what to do.

I will be very thankful for this.

Respectfully,
A.

ANSWER:

Many of those who took part in the freedom struggle are drawn to take a look at liberated Russia. But not everyone can do so. This is also the position of the writer, who has obligations to his wife. She is an American, she has her family here, so how can she leave her home and go to a strange country? The writer must take this into consideration. Besides, while the terrible battles are still raging, there can be no discussion about visiting Russia.

Many Jews were on the barricades during the great revolution in Russia. Chaim Weizmann's mother had another son Abraham, who was a revolutionary, and she once said, "If Abraham wins we will live in Russia in peace and security, and if Chaim wins we'll go to Palestine and live in peace and security there." Chaim won, and of course became the first President of Israel. Abraham has not yet won. Soviet Russia is still a prison for the Jews.

1919

Dear Editor,

I find myself in a desperate position and I turn to you in hopes that you will advise me what to do.

I am thirty-six years old, and I came here several years ago from Russian Poland, because I couldn't earn enough for bread for my wife and our two children there. The first few years here I struggled and earned barely enough to survive. Still, I saved penny by penny and finally sent steamship tickets for my wife and children, whom I had left at home.

The day I sent out the tickets was a holiday for me. I was happy that I'd soon be with my family, I'd have a home like other people, and not have to sit at strangers' tables.

But it turned out differently than I thought. I was terribly disappointed, because a few weeks later the tickets were returned to me, with a letter from my wife saying she didn't need me and didn't want to come. I couldn't understand why such a crazy idea should come to her and I asked what had happened to her. She repeated in her answer that she would not come to me.

Right after that the World War broke out, and I didn't hear any more from my wife and children. When the war was over and sad news began to arrive from the destroyed towns in Poland, I waited for some word of my family. Since I live in Philadelphia, I traveled to New York to make inquiries in various places.

But I was not able to get any news about my wife and children. I was told that they must be dead, because if they were alive I would have heard from them by now.

I even sent money to my wife at the old address, but it came back. I took this as proof that my family was really dead.

In time I began to go out with a girl, and I told her the whole story about my family. She also believed that my wife and children were no longer living. So we got married and we now have a child.

But recently I was reading in the *Forverts* a list of the unfortunate, displaced people who are looking for their relatives in America, and suddenly I was as if paralyzed. I saw that my wife had "arisen from the dead" and was seeking me and asking for my help.

What's to be done now? I beg you to answer me immediately.

The Despairing One

ANSWER:

It is actually not the writer's fault that he is in such a dilemma. From the earlier letters he received from his wife, it was clear that she didn't love him and didn't want to come to him. However he must try to help her in her need, and then get a legal divorce from her.

1920

Worthy Editor,

This letter is written to you by a young widow. I was married during wartime, and ten weeks after the wedding my husband was drafted. He was shipped to France, he saw action in the battles, and my anxiety was great. But my joy was even greater when the war ended and my husband was alive and unhurt.

When my husband left the battlefields, before they sent him home, he wrote me letters that breathed of joy and hope. "Soon,

soon we will be together, and we will never part again," he wrote. Suddenly a telegram from the government brought me the shocking news that my dear husband had died of pneumonia. It is impossible to describe what I lived through, but life goes on. I work and earn a living, but I am lonely.

Now it's like this: In the house where I live I met a young man whose wife died last year and left him with a child. I became friendly with him, and he suggested that I marry him. I love his child and feel sympathy for it, because I, too, was left a young orphan. It is a good match for me, and I want to marry the young widower but one thing holds me back.

I heard that the government is going to bring back to America all the soldiers who fell on the battlefields in Europe. The next of kin of these soldiers will then have the opportunity of burying them and erecting headstones at their graves. No one knows when it will be done, but I wouldn't want to get married before they bring my dead husband home. I want to have a funeral and provide a headstone for him.

The young man, however, wants us to get married now, so his child can have a home as soon as possible. But the memory of my husband keeps me from taking this step. Some of my friends advise me to leave the money that the burial and the headstone will cost with his family, and they will take care of everything, but my heart won't let me do this.

I beg you to give your opinion about this problem and answer quickly.

Respectfully,
The Young Widow

ANSWER:

There is some talk in the War Department about bringing home from France the fallen American soldiers and giving them a burial here with full military honors. When this will occur is not yet known. It is possible that they may never bring them home. Therefore it would be advisable for the writer of this letter to consider the suggestion of her friends, which is quite practical.

1920

Dear Editor,

I write you this letter because I want to hear your opinion about the behavior of a woman I am acquainted with, who belongs to progressive groups and considers herself a radical.

Not long ago the couple invited me to their home and I spent a pleasant evening with them. When the time came to eat supper, everyone went into the dining room to sit down at the table, and the poor woman who works for them ate in the kitchen.

Since I know the couple and I know they consider themselves radical people, I wondered why the servant didn't eat at the table along with everyone. I took the liberty of telling my friend that she ought to ask the woman in to eat with us in the dining room, because it wasn't right for her to sit alone in the kitchen. Then my friend answered me that it has to be this way, that the woman who works for them must eat separately.

For me, this was not the right answer and it seems that one of us does not understand the meaning of ethics and morals of the Socialistic standpoint. Therefore I ask you to explain to us which one is right.

With Socialistic regards,
A Reader

ANSWER:

We are in agreement with the writer, and not with her friend. Progressive people should not discriminate between the servant and the members of the family. When everyone eats in the dining room and the maid is left sitting in the kitchen, they are wronging her because this is degrading.

1920

Worthy Editor,

We ask you to print this letter as soon as possible and render a judgment on the question that has come up in our society. Thus you can help us avoid a split in the Relief Society of the *landsleit* of S——— [the name of the city was given here]. If our organization is disbanded, the unfortunate war victims in our home town in Europe will suffer.

Among our *landsleit* there are wealthy people as well as poor ones. The "alrightniks" who worked their way up here in America are those who in our home town didn't have enough bread to satisfy their hunger. The men who were wealthy back home, who stood with their silver-trimmed prayer shawls by the eastern wall of the *shul*, alas, are poor here.

The wealthy ones organized the Relief Society and are the officers—president, treasurer. In a word, they have all the honors which we do not begrudge them because "He who has the might has the right." They do, in fact, give the greatest donations for our brothers across the ocean, and everybody admits they deserve the honor. But disputes have arisen for the following reason:

Our officers passed a resolution that the names of all those who contributed to the Relief Fund and the amounts each one gave should be read aloud at each meeting. Certain of the *landsleit*, especially the ones who were once wealthy, are ashamed to hear their small donations called out from the platform, because this way their poverty is publicized. They can't stand it, because in our home town they were the greatest philanthropists.

So what do our former rich men who are now poor do? They do not come to the meetings. It may soon come to the point where our Relief Society will consist only of those who are well off, and our brothers and sisters in Europe will suffer.

There are quarrels at our meetings. The officers insist that reading the lists publicly is necessary because certain *landsleit* who can give large contributions for the Relief Fund get away with small donations. Calling out the names is a challenge to do their duty for the war victims.

We are depending on your decision.

Respectfully,
A Committee from our Relief Society

ANSWER:

It is very unpleasant when there is a rivalry for honors in public affairs, especially when they deal with helping war victims. Across the ocean, Jewish blood is being spilled, there are plenty of hooligans lying in wait for Jews, to pull their beards, beat them up, and here you are fighting for glory and want the whole world to know how much this one and that one contributed.

It is commendable that the successful *landsleit* give with a generous hand to help the unfortunates, but it is not necessary to announce how much each one gives at the meetings. It is important to consider the feelings of the impoverished, former wealthy men who cannot give large sums of money here in America.

One of the inducements to attend a Bonds for Israel dinner is the statement on the invitation, "No names will be called," which means that the individual purchasers will not be announced from the platform.

1921

Worthy Editor,

I am a widow who was left without an income, and with the help of friends I opened a small restaurant on the East Side.

All kinds of people came into my restaurant, and among them was a boy who was attracted to my youngest daughter. She was quite young, but he talked her into marrying him. I saw that the young man was not for her, but I couldn't do anything to stop the marriage.

After the wedding I found out soon enough that my son-in-law was lazy and didn't want to work. My foolish young daughter lacked the necessities of life, but since I am a mother I helped and shared my food with her.

To my misfortune, my "dear" son-in-law even talked my daughter into believing in Christian Science. My young, inexperienced, foolish child obeyed him and became a follower of the new doctrine. She began to believe that illnesses can be cured without doctors, and because of it, she lost her first child. When the child got sick, instead of calling the doctor, she tried to cure it with prayer, and the poor child died.

Now my daughter has a second child, and when it gets sick she "heals" it with prayers and with talking to it, according to the "prescriptions" of Christian Science. I am afraid that the fate of my second grandchild will be the same as the first. My son-in-law earns very little and he tries to persuade my daughter that, just as one can live without medicine, so one can live without food. She even gives her last few cents to the Church, believing that she thus assures herself of a "world to come."

My daughter comes to me only when she is starving or when she needs money. She and her husband don't care about me and do everything they can against me. It has gone so far that they haven't even had their son circumcised.

I had to give up the restaurant, because I didn't have the strength to run it alone. Now I can hardly earn enough for myself, yet I still have to help my daughter. But I wonder whether I should continue to help her, when I cannot influence her to turn away from her foolish way of life. I beg you to advise me.

Thank you in advance,
A Mother

ANSWER:

In our opinion, the mother does not have to give money to her daughter for the Church. Her daughter and son-in-law do not deserve the support of a mother who is a poor widow, barely able to take care of her own needs.

1923

Worthy Mr. Editor,

I was born in a small town in Russia and my mother brought me up alone, because I had lost my father when I was a child. My dear mother used all her energies to give me a proper education.

A pogrom broke out and my mother was the first victim of the blood bath. They spared no one, and no one was left for me. But that wasn't enough for the murderers, they robbed me of my honor. I begged them to kill me instead, but they let me live to suffer and grieve.

After that there were long days and nights of loneliness and grief. I was alone, despondent and homeless, until relatives in America brought me over. But my wounded heart found no cure here either. Here I am lonely, too, and no one cares. I am dejected, without a ray of hope, because all my former dreams for the future are shattered.

A few months ago, however, I met a young man, a refined and decent man. It didn't take long before we fell in love. He has already proposed marriage and he is now waiting for my answer.

I want to marry this man, but I keep putting off giving him an answer because I can't tell him the secret that weighs on my heart and bothers my conscience. I have no rest and am almost going out of my mind. When my friend comes to hear my answer, I want to tell him everything. Let him know all; I've bottled up the pain inside me long enough. Let him hear all and then decide. But I have no words and can tell him nothing.

I hope you will answer and advise me what I can do.

I thank you,
A Reader

ANSWER:

In the pogroms, in the great Jewish disasters, this misfortune befell many Jewish girls like you. But you must not feel guilty and not be so dejected, because you are innocent. A man who can understand and sympathize can be told everything. If your friend is one of these people and he really loves you, he will cherish you even after he learns your secret.

Since we do not know your friend, it is hard for us to advise you whether to tell him everything now, or not. In this matter you must take more responsibility on yourself. You know the man, and you must know, more or less, if he will be able to understand.

1924

Worthy Editor,

I am a married man, and I live with my wife and two children in a city not too far from New York. We lived peacefully and happily, but now our house has turned into a Gehenna. Hear the reason:

When the World War ended, my sister wrote me from New York that I should bring our mother over from the old country. I thought it would be better for her not to come to America, because I had been sending her enough money to live on. But my sister bombarded me with letters and assured me that she would keep Mother with her and that I should just bring her here. I listened to my sister, spent over five hundred dollars, and brought Mother to New York. We were overjoyed when she

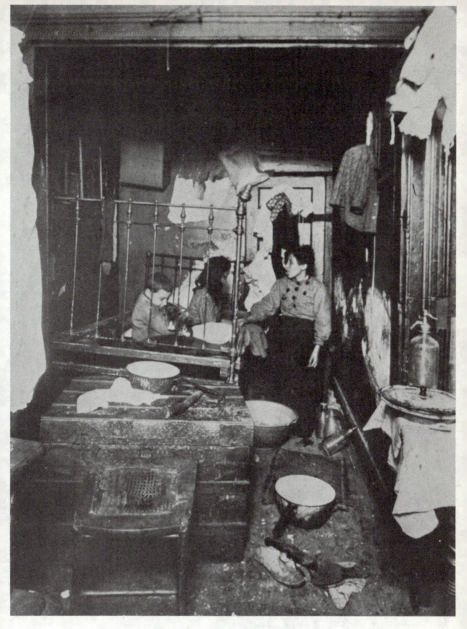

Tenement rear bedroom, c. 1910.

Saluting the flag at school, 1890.

Child labor on the Lower East Side, 1910.

Taking work home, c. 1910. Many women workers took their children with them to the shop.

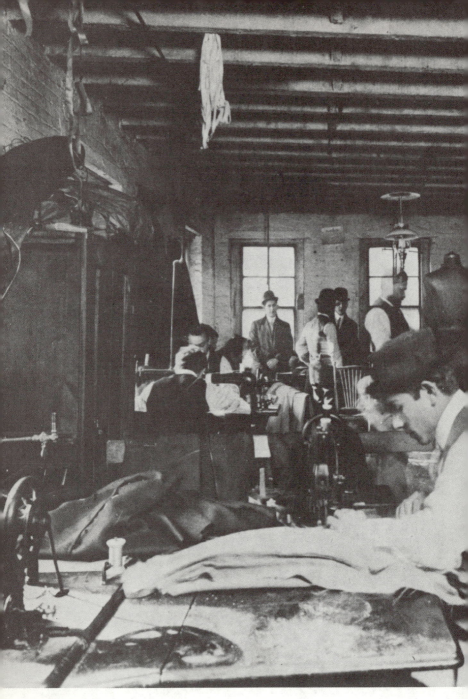

LEFT: Jewish garment worker at his shop, 1915. RIGHT: Woman carrying piecework for home manufacture, 1909. Many homes had sewing machines so such homework was possible.

The garment carrier, c. 1910 — a common Lower East Side street scene of the period.

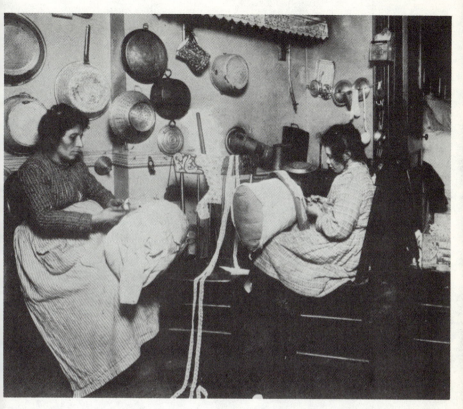

Making lace embroidery at home, 1910. The garment would then be returned to the factory for manufacture.

The terrible Triangle Shirtwaist Factory fire, 1911. This is a corner of the building's ninth floor looking out on Greene Street. One hundred and forty six people died in this tragic fire.

Clothing workers' strike, 1909. Most laborers in the garment trade were either Jewish or Italian.

came, and after that I often sent money to my sister for keeping Mother with her.

Time passed, and suddenly I got a letter from my mother, saying that I should have pity on her and take her to my house, because her daughter didn't want to keep her any more and she was out on the street. Well, I took her to my home, but it's no good, because my wife doesn't want her in the house either. Now I want to place my mother in a Home, but she doesn't want to go. She would rather see me leave my wife and children because of her. If not, she says, I should give her five hundred dollars, and she'll go back to Europe. She doesn't want to go to her old home, but to another town, since she's ashamed to tell people that she couldn't stay with her children.

I am not a rich man, but I would give her the five hundred dollars already, so that she could go home. But how can I let such an old woman go back to Poland? And what will she do there all alone? I have two other sisters there, but Mother never got along with them either and can't stay with them.

What shall I do? My wife is very loyal and I love her and my children. I love my mother too and my heart aches for her. I beg you to give me some advice and answer quickly.

Respectfully,
C.N.

ANSWER:

The best thing for you would be to rent a room somewhere for your mother and support her there. Such a capricious woman can get along better with strangers than with her own family. But if she insists on going back to Poland, you must first write to your sisters who live there to hear their opinion about it. It is possible she would actually feel better there. Meanwhile you should get a room for her so that she does not have to remain with you.

1925

Dear Editor,

I have been a *Forverts* reader for the past twenty years, and I feel I have the right to ask you to print my letter.

First I want to introduce myself. I am the widow of Z.H. [full name was given], who was murdered by Negro bandits who held him up on a Saturday night in his store in Harlem [date and address of store were given]. At that time you wrote in the *Forverts* that my husband was killed because he did not understand the orders of the burglars. I want to correct you here. My husband understood very well what they said, but it was his principle to fight them off.

My husband, with the help of our son H—— and of his clerk, had driven the Negroes out of the store and he started to yell, "Police," at the top of his lungs. This angered the murderers and they killed him. I want to remark that my husband always said he would never stand for robbery by holdup men.

I beg you earnestly to correct the error in your worthy newspaper. But this is not the only reason for writing you this letter. I want to ask you about something else.

I am a progressive person and do not believe in superstition. Yet lately my thoughts are disturbed over something I dreamed a night before my husband's death, and I would like to hear your opinion on this. I dreamed I was standing between two walls and couldn't get out. With great effort I finally tore myself free and went into the dining room, where I saw that the windows were draped in black. I began to scream, demanding to know why they made my dining room so dark, and the scream awakened me.

Later I forgot about it, but when the policeman came to tell me the terrible news about my husband's death, I immediately recalled the dream and it follows me at every step. I keep thinking about the dream and about my husband's terrible death. I ask you to tell me your opinion of my dream, and maybe that will calm me.

> I thank you in advance,
> The Widow

ANSWER:
The report of the holdup was written up in the newspaper in the heat of the moment, as soon as the news came from the Police Department. And, as can happen, some discrepancies crept in. We are therefore satisfied that printing this letter will correct the errors.

Your dream is no more than coincidence that has little connection with the misfortune that befell you. In human life there are many such occurrences, and you should not take them seriously. You must try to calm yourself and try to forget about it.

1926

Worthy Editor,

We live in a small town in the country where we are the only Jewish family, and we earn a good living here. So all is well, apparently. But we have four daughters, all of them ready for marriage, and there is no one here with whom to make a match. We wanted to send them to a big city, but they don't want to go without Mother and Father. They want us to give up the business, sell everything, and move to another city. But we have no desire to break up our home and give up our good life. It's not easy, in our declining years, to go seek a living elsewhere, when we have such a good business here.

But what doesn't one do for children? Here it's impossible to marry off a girl, because there are no Jews, only Gentiles. Our daughters are fine girls. They are always in the store and behave decently. The question is, however, how will it end? We beg you to advise us.

Your Country Readers

ANSWER:

In order to advise them, we would have to be well acquainted with their family life, their circumstances, and the character of the parents and their children. We can only tell them that many Jewish families that are in the same position leave the small towns for the sake of their children. Others, on the other hand, remain where they are.

In such circumstances it is better not to rely on advice of others but on themselves.

A Jew who has three or four daughters is in bad shape. In the small towns of the South the Jew has discovered a system. He sends his daughters up to Philadelphia or Boston or to Atlanta where she can meet Jewish boys. The boys stay home and enter the father's store or become professionals, and some of them wind up marrying shikses.

1926

Worthy Mr. Editor,

Be so kind as to give us your opinion in your worthy newspaper as to whether it is a custom or a law among Jews that a suicide must be buried by the cemetery fence. I don't know why a suicide should be regarded as an outcast and a shame to society.

A widow who was a member in our society committed suicide, not, God forbid, over an unhappy love affair or other silly reasons, but because of poverty and trouble. I, as president of the society, allowed her to be buried in the proper row according to our constitution. Now many members are criticizing my actions, but that's not all. One member, whose wife's grave happens to be next to the suicide's, went right out and bought a plot in another cemetery. Now he demands permission to take his wife's body out of the grave, because he is ashamed to have her lie near a suicide.

Since this matter must be handled soon at a meeting of the society, I ask you to answer me as soon as possible.

I remain, respectfully,
The President

ANSWER:

It's not enough that in her despair the unfortunate woman was driven to end her tragic life, but inconsiderate people come to insult her even now after death. Protests should be made against the custom of burying suicides by the fence. The man whom it doesn't suit to have his wife lie near a suicide is uncivilized. He should be scolded soundly and the president praised because he acted correctly.

1928

Worthy Editor,

I consider myself a progressive woman who thinks there should be no difference between Jews and Christians. Years ago when I was a girl and sometimes heard that parents would not allow their children to marry a Christian, I maintained that they should not interfere. I believed that a fine Christian was as good as a fine Jew.

Now, however, when my daughter has fallen in love with a Gentile, I have become one of those mothers who interferes because I am against this match. I am not one of those fanatic parents who warn their children that they will disown them because of it, but I'm trying with goodness to influence my daughter to break up with the boy.

My daughter argues with me: "Why? You always used to say

that all people are equal." She is educated, she knows how to talk to me, and often I have no answers to her arguments. But I feel this is no match for my daughter. Her friend comes here often, and as a person he appeals to me, but not as a husband for her.

I don't know how to explain it. He is intelligent, quiet and gentle, but somehow his nature and his way of thinking are different from that of a Jew. His parents are American Yankees, never miss a Sunday at church and speak with reverence of President Coolidge. When I think that they might become my in-laws and their son my daughter's husband, I tremble. I feel —a mother's heart feels—that my daughter could never get used to these people.

When one is young and in love, one is in the clouds and sees no flaws. But when love cools down, she will see it's no good. I see it in advance. True, it could happen that she could marry a Jewish man and after the wedding not be able to stand him. But with a Jew it's still different.

I would very much like to hear your opinion about this.

Respectfully,
A Mother

ANSWER:

You yourself answered everything in your letter, and our opinion is the same as yours. Your daughter should also understand that the match is not a good one. But she is infatuated with the young man. And when one is in love, then all the sensible arguments are worthless.

1930

Worthy Editor,

A short time ago my friends and relatives discussed the role of the matchmaker in present-day society. The discussion arose in connection with my sister, a woman in her thirties who has been a widow for about ten years.

My sister had a good education in Europe. In America she graduated from high school and had two years of college. We in the family are proud of her because she is smart, well educated, and has a fine character. But it hurts us to see her wasting her best years alone. We would very much like to have her remarry. Since she is involved in business and seldom goes out, I expressed an opinion that she ought to go to a *shadkhan*, who could easily arrange a match for her.

My sister answered that anyone with self-respect wouldn't go to a matchmaker, because that seemed to her like going on the slave market. Marriage to her means the union of two people bound by friendship and love.

Then a discussion developed on whether an intelligent, progressive person should go to a matchmaker. Some expressed the opinion that, when a person cannot find a match for himself, there's nothing wrong if he marries through a *shadkhan*, since this is no obstacle to happiness.

Others agreed with my sister. They argued that going to a matchmaker was only for ignorant people in remote towns in Europe. A modern intelligent person should not go to be weighed and measured like a cow at the fair.

So we decided to leave it up to you, worthy Editor. May educated, progressive people go to a *shadkhan*? We, and especially my sister, are very interested to hear your opinion.

> With thanks and regards,
> A Reader in the name of A Group

ANSWER:

It depends on how a person feels about this, because consulting a matchmaker has nothing to do with education or enlightenment. One person might consider it like a fair where cattle are sold. Another person has an altogether different opinion because a *shadkhan* nowadays does not match up brides and grooms sight unseen. He just introduces people so that they can get acquainted. If they like each other they can fall in love. Couldn't the parks, Coney Island beaches, or a dance hall where people meet, also be considered matchmakers?

The shadkhan was a marriage broker. He brought together boys and girls for the purpose of matrimony. Thousands of marriages were the result of the shadkhan's work. The shadkhan wore a derby and carried an umbrella, and he was a familiar figure on the East Side of New York. The shadkhan did not match brides and grooms sight unseen. He discussed the matter with the families of both parties. For the first "date" he might give each of the parties a ticket to a Yiddish stage show with seats of course next to each other. This would give them both a chance to look each other over and decide whether they wanted to see each other again. They may have had another date to a movie or to an ice cream parlor. And then the girl's family invited him to dinner on a Friday night and if he accepted it looked like a deal. The shadkhan then gave the terms of the engagement, the dowry if any, and the contract was signed.

There is no doubt that the percentage of successful marriages as the result of the shadkhan's efforts were not any more or less than those marriages outside the shadkhan's domain.

1932

Worthy Mr. Editor,

I have been married to my husband twenty-three years and we always had a fine family life. Recently, however, something terrible happened to destroy our happiness.

I believed in my husband the way a religious Jew believes in God, and now my faith in him is shattered. Nine months ago I found out accidentally that my husband has a mistress. At first I didn't want to believe it, but when I began to look further and investigate, I found out about things that made my hair stand on end.

I found out that it went so far that my husband bought or rented a house for his mistress, that he supports her in luxury and goes to her quite often. I even know which days he's with her.

When I found out everything, I naturally made a terrible scene. But that didn't scare my husband. On the contrary, he began to threaten to leave me altogether. And his mistress warned me that she would take out a summons against me, because I called her names and talked against her.

Now I question whether to apply for a divorce. I know he still sees her often, and if I get the divorce he will be the winner and not I, because then he'll surely marry his mistress. But to go on living with him is impossible.

What's to be done? I beg you to answer me soon.

Respectfully,
Deceived

ANSWER:

If everything is actually as you describe it, it is easy to understand why you cannot and will not live with your husband. But perhaps this is more a situation that comes from your imagination than an actual fact. We would like to hear what your husband has to say regarding the accusation and we expect that he will write to us about your letter.

1932

Dear Editor,

I am an immigrant from Russia, my wife is American-born, and we are both freethinkers. We have two grown children, a son and a daughter, who know they are Jews but never saw any signs of religion or holidays in our home. Even *Yom Kippur* is just another day to us. For the last twenty years we've lived among Christians and we socialize with them. Our children also go around with Gentiles.

Some time ago a Christian girl began to come to our house, seemingly to visit our daughter, but it was no secret to us that she was after our twenty-three-year-old son, with whom she was friendly. We said nothing about it, because we wouldn't have minded having her for a daughter-in-law.

Once the girl invited our son to a party at her house where all the other guests were Gentiles. They were all having a good time until one of the guests, whether in jest or earnest, began to make fun of Jews. I don't know what happened there, but I am sure they didn't mean to hurt my son, because none of them, not even his girl friend, knew that he is Jewish. But he was insulted and told the girl so. Then he told her that he is Jewish and this was a surprise to her.

My son left the party immediately and from that day on he is changed. He began to ask questions about religion, debated with me about things that formerly hadn't interested him. He wanted to know where I was born, how many Jews there are in the world, why the religious don't eat pork, where the hatred of Jews came from, and on and on. He was not satisfied with my short answers but began to read books looking for more information. My son also berated me for not giving him a Jewish upbringing.

His Gentile girl friend came to beg him to forgive her. She cried and explained that it was not her fault, but he didn't want to have anything to do with her because, it seems, he was deeply insulted. His head was filled with one thought, Jewishness. He found Jewish friends, he was drawn into a Zionist club and they worked on him so that he has come to me with a suggestion that I give up the business and we all go to Palestine. And since he sees that I am not about to go, he's getting ready to go alone.

At first we took it as a joke, but we see now that he's taking it very seriously. Well, my going is out of the question, I am not that crazy. But what can be done about him? I'm willing to give in to his whim. I'm sure that in Palestine he'll sober up and realize that not everyone who is Jewish must live in Palestine. My wife is carrying on terribly; what do I mean, allowing my son to travel to a wild country where Arabs shoot Jews? She says we should not give him the money for the trip. But our son says he will find a way to reach the Jewish Homeland.

My wife and I are very anxious to hear your opinion.

Respectfully,
A Reader

ANSWER:

Your son is a very sensitive and thinking person. Since he is an adult you must let him go his way and do what he wants to do.

Many letters from Russian Jews indicate that they have become Zionists. Their attitude is that they see Zionism as the means of abolishing the "abnormal" position of the Jew, an instrument whereby he might become a man like other people.

This recalls a statement in Theodor Herzl's Diary. "We must have an army with officers with the red stripe running down their trouser leg, and a navy, even if it has only one gunboat. These are the values the world understands."

Chaim Nachman Bialik, the great Hebrew poet, said it in a different way. "When the first Jewish prostitute is arrested by the first Jewish policeman and sentenced by the first Jewish judge, we can consider ourselves a sovereign state."

1932

Worthy Editor,

Though I am only a simple tailor, my mind is not occupied only with scissors and needle. I also like to read, to learn, and I have great respect for educated people. I am a man of middle age with grown children, and I have been a reader of your newspaper for the past twenty years.

All my life I strove to give my children a good upbringing because I wanted them to be serious, educated people. And I am appealing to you for advice about one son who will soon finish high school. My son distinguished himself in chemistry all through high school and got the highest marks in that subject. He is absorbed in it with all his heart and soul. He studies day and night, carries on experiments, and never gets tired.

This pleases me very much, because when someone studies a subject he loves, he can, in time, achieve something and maybe even become great in that field. Who knows? But in spite of this joy I'm unhappy. Why? Because I read in the Jewish newspapers that in this profession there is no future for Jewish graduates. I read that a graduate chemist cannot get a position in a large firm if he is a Jew.

I didn't want to believe that in America, in such a free land, it was really so. But recently I met a graduate, a Jewish chemist, and he confirmed that what I read was true.

As yet there are no large Jewish firms that hire chemists, and among the non-Jewish firms there is a sort of understanding to keep Jews out of this profession which has a great future.

I don't expect you to be able to help me but I think you might be better acquainted with the situation and you can advise me whether I should let my son continue his studies in this field. Maybe I should make my son a tailor.

I thank you in advance for printing my letter and for your answer.

Your reader,
S.G.

ANSWER:

We maintain that your son should study the profession in which he is so strongly interested. In spite of all difficulties, he will, in time, find his way in life.

1933

Worthy Editor,

I have been a reader of the *Forverts* all the nineteen years I've been in America, and I can tell you that here, in this country, I have not yet had one quiet minute. I am the mother of six children, and this alone is enough worry and bother to a mother. But that's not all. The main thing is that I always had to work to provide bread for my children. My husband is a janitor and earns very little.

But I have not come to you to complain about my hard work. It's about an altogether different thing. From my hard labor, I have saved up several hundred dollars, and naturally this is not a secret from my husband. But now he wants me to give him the money. And what do you think he wants it for? To buy an orange plantation in Palestine. Actually, he already bought the plantation and made the down payment and he wants us to go there to live. He wants the money for a ticket so he can go to Palestine first by himself.

I argue with him that if this little money I've saved will be spent for travel expenses, then what will we do there later? How will we make a living with our six children? And if he goes alone it'll be hard for me to get along without him here. I have no desire whatsoever to go, but I am afraid he'll talk the older children into going too.

I beg you to give me your opinion about his plan to go live in Palestine. He has never seen and doesn't know how to work on a plantation.

Your reader,
S.J.B.

ANSWER:

The writer and her husband should go to the American Economic Committee for Palestine at 17 East Forty-second Street, New York. There they can get the necessary information about the production of oranges in Palestine. Also they can tell this man whether he is suited for this kind of work.

But if the woman absolutely does not want to leave America, the man should consider her and should not break up his home.

1933

Worthy Editor,

I am sure that the problem I'm writing about affects many Jewish homes. It deals with immigrant parents and their American-born children.

My parents, who have been readers of your paper for years, came from Europe. They have been here in this country over thirty years and were married twenty-eight years ago. They have five sons, and I am one of them. The oldest of us is twenty-seven and the youngest twenty-one.

We are all making a decent living. One of us works for the State Department. A second is a manager in a large store, two are in business, and the youngest is studying law. Our parents do not need our help because my father has a good job.

We, the five brothers, always speak English to each other. Our parents know English too, but they speak only Yiddish, not just among themselves but to us too, and even to our American friends who come to visit us. We beg them not to speak Yiddish in the presence of our friends, since they can speak English, but they don't want to. It's a sort of stubbornness on their part, and a great deal of quarreling goes on between our parents and ourselves because of it.

Their answer is: "Children, we ask you not to try to teach us how to talk to people. We are older than you."

Imagine, even when we go with our father to buy something in a store on Fifth Avenue, New York, he insists on speaking Yiddish. We are not ashamed of our parents, God forbid, but they ought to know where it's proper and where it's not. If they talk Yiddish among themselves at home, or to us, it's bad enough, but among strangers and Christians? Is that nice? It looks as if they're doing it to spite us. Petty spats grow out of it. They want to keep only to their old ways and don't want to take up our new ways.

We beg you, friend Editor, to express your opinion on this question, and if possible send us your answer in English, because we can't read Yiddish.

Accept our thanks for your answer, which we expect soon,

Respectfully,
I. and the Four Brothers

ANSWER:

We see absolutely no crime in the parents' speaking Yiddish to their sons. The Yiddish language is dear to them and they want to speak in that language to their children and all who understand it. It may also be that they are ashamed to speak their imperfect English among strangers so they prefer to use their mother tongue.

From the letter, we get the impression that the parents are not fanatics, and with their speaking Yiddish they are not out to spite the children. But it would certainly not be wrong if the parents were to speak English too, to the children. People should and must learn the language of their country.

1933

Worthy Editor,

Though my husband is a Zionist and I used to be a Bund-ist, we have already celebrated our silver wedding anniversary and lived the quarter century happily together.

We have five children, with whom all parents would consider themselves blessed. We gave them a good education, sent them to college, and they are all good, bright and cultured. We are in business, and until the depression we made a good living.

Two of our children are already married. One boy, eighteen years old, is studying at City College, one works in a department store with a college diploma in his pocket and earns such poor wages it's a shame to talk about it. But what can one do, when even this job was hard for him to get? And our twenty-one-year-old daughter did something that my husband, the Zionist, can-not stand. It's about her that I am writing this letter to you.

Our daughter graduated from college with high honors, but this did not help her find a job. She could not find work for a long time, but two months ago she got a very good job in an insurance company, and she brings home a check for thirty-five dollars every week. We should be satisfied, yet our world has turned upside down since she got the job.

My husband is very upset, because in order to get the job my daughter had to give her religion as Episcopalian. If they had known she was Jewish they wouldn't have hired her. She doesn't have typically Jewish features, and from her appearance she can be taken for a Christian. One of my sons says she also had to get a recommendation from a priest, because lately many Jewish girls say they are Christians in order to get a job. The priest's recommendation is the only way to assure the boss that he is not being fooled.

Our whole house is topsy-turvy. My husband insists that by

all means she should give up the job. Our whole family is now divided into two sides. One side feels that our daughter has not committed a crime and hasn't wronged anyone. As far as her own conscience goes, it's not so terrible. Would going around jobless and having to come to her father or mother for a dollar be better?

I feel that I, myself, wouldn't do it, but I sympathize with my daughter. But my husband is terribly upset about the whole thing. We would like your opinion about our daughter's actions.

Your troubled readers,
F. and G.

ANSWER:

The father is entirely right in his stand against his daughter's actions, and his feelings about it are not necessarily caused by his being a Zionist. A Jewish father, whether he is a Socialist or a freethinker, would also be against having his daughter posing as a Christian in order to get a job. But the fact is that the girl is already twenty-one years old. She certainly doesn't deserve a compliment for her dishonest behavior, but she has the right to act as she wishes.

Companies that do not hire Jews, though they have a large Jewish patronage, should be condemned.

Discrimination against the Jews in industry still exists to a certain extent to this day. A few years ago I inquired of the largest corporations in America whether this was so and they were frank with me. They said that there were Jews in their laboratories at the home office but that they could not promote a Jew to regional offices. Life in these regional offices around the country is based on community social involvement and because the Jews cannot get into the Gentile country clubs they are barred from these jobs.

Jewish graduates from business schools in the early days found it extremely difficult to find jobs. Many of them claimed they were Episcopalian or Catholic. My own sister wore a cross to

*work in an insurance company in uptown New York. She re-
moved the cross nightly on her way home.*

1935

Dear Editor,

Since I cannot write Yiddish, I have asked our neighbor,
a devoted friend of the family, to write this letter for me.

I am twenty-five years old, married to a respectable man, a
cab driver, who earns very little, but I am satisfied because I
never dreamed of riches and luxury. We have a nice home and
I see to it that the house is clean, neat and pleasant. We
have a child, two years old, pretty and smart, and she is our
whole life.

My husband doesn't drink, smoke or gamble, and whatever
he earns he brings home and hands over to me. We love each
other and lead a happy family life. The thing is that in our
life there is a "But." I am not Jewish but Christian, or, as
my mother-in-law says, a *shikse*, and it's trouble.

My mother-in-law embitters my life. She comes to my home
every day, but only for the sake of her grandchild, whom she
loves dearly. And she comes every Sunday with her own auto-
mobile and takes all of us for a ride. But it's far from being
good.

My husband loves me, but he also loves his mother very
much. It's fine to love your mother, but his love for her is like
a baby's for its mother. My husband is tall, handsome, well
built, but when his mother comes he turns into a child that
clings to her apron. When she comes they kiss and hug each
other, she pats his head, deplores the fact that he looks bad
when he really looks fine.

To me, she insinuates that I have ruined her son because,
if not for me, he would have married a beautiful and wealthy
Jewish girl. Usually I hear her out and keep silent, but when
I occasionally answer back with a sharp word, she starts to

cry. Then she complains to my husband and there's havoc in the house. She even believes it's my fault that he's no more than a cab driver, because nobody in the family wants to do anything for him because he married a *shikse*.

When I talk to my mother about this, she tells me I must treat my mother-in-in-law with respect and in time everything will turn our for the best. I am a high school graduate, I am also not ugly. I am on good terms with my husband's brothers and sisters, and I would like very much to be close to my mother-in-law but she doesn't encourage it. I am only afraid she may succeed in upsetting our family life. I beg you to suggest how I should deal with the situation.

> With great respect,
> Deborah

ANSWER:
The writer, who is an intelligent woman, understands the special circumstances that are entailed in her family life. She must consider these circumstances and follow the logical advice of her mother.

1938

Dear Editor,

I come to you with my family problem because I think you are the only one who can give me practical advice. I am a man in my fifties, and I came to America when I was very young. I don't have to tell you how hard life was for a "greenhorn" in those times. I suffered plenty. But that didn't keep me from falling in love with a girl from my home town and marrying her.

I harnessed myself to the wagon of family life and pulled with all my strength. My wife was faithful and she gave me a hand in pulling the wagon. The years flew fast and before we looked around we were parents of four children who brightened and sweetened our lives.

The children were dear and smart and we gave them an education that was more than we could afford. They went to college, became professionals, and are well established.

Suddenly I feel as if the floor has collapsed under my feet. I don't know how to express it, but the fact that my children are well educated and have outgrown me makes me feel bad. I can't talk to them about my problems and they can't talk to me about theirs. It's as if there were a deep abyss that divides us.

People envy me my good, fine, educated children but (I am ashamed to admit it) I often think it might be better for me if they were not so well educated, but ordinary workingmen, like me. Then we would have more in common. I have no education, because my parents were poor, and in the old country they couldn't give me the opportunities that I could give my children. Here, in America, I didn't have time and my mind wasn't on learning in the early years when I had to work hard.

That is my problem. I want to hear your opinion about it. I enclose my full name and address, but please do not print it. I will sign as,

                              Disappointed

ANSWER:

It is truly a pleasure to have such children, and the father can really be envied. But he must not feel he has nothing in common with them any longer, because they have more education than he. There should be no chasm between father and children, and if there is, perhaps he himself created it.

In thousands of Jewish immigrant homes such educated children have grown up, and many of them remain close to their parents. Also there is no reason why the writer of this letter shouldn't be able to talk to his fine, good children about various problems, even though they are professionals and have outdistanced him in their education.

1939

Dear Editor,

I haven't been in the country very long, and I ask you to clarify a certain matter for me. I was brought here by my brother-in-law, with whom I get along very well, but we have a difference of opinion on one thing. I think I'm right, my brother-in-law believes he's right, so I decided to ask you. This is the problem:

A short time ago I had occasion to ride on a train and I took along the *Forverts* to read on the way. My brother-in-law said it wasn't nice, that it wasn't fitting to read a Jewish newspaper on the train. Even though I'm still a "greenhorn" in America, my Americanized brother-in-law's statement didn't have any effect on me.

I know America is a free country and the Jew is not oppressed here as in other lands, so why should I have to be ashamed of my language here? I certainly would not read a Jewish paper in a train in Germany or Poland. And do you know why? Because there they would beat me up for such *chutzpa*. Here, in America, though, I don't have to be afraid of anyone.

A few days later I had to take the subway somewhere with a friend and I noticed that he wouldn't leave the house until he finished reading his Yiddish newspaper. I remarked that he could take the paper along and read it on the way. And listen to this answer: "I've been in this country seventeen years and never yet read a Jewish paper on the subway." When I asked him why, he avoided giving me a direct answer.

I would like to hear your opinion about this.

With thanks,
The "Greenhorn"

ANSWER:

No, people should not be ashamed to read a Yiddish newspaper in the train or subway. Many are not ashamed to do so. One should only be ashamed of something bad or not respectable. And something not respectable should not even be done in secret. The *Talmud* says, "That which should not be done hidden in a closed room is also not permitted in the open."

It is well known that our mother tongue has already gained an honorable position among the world languages. The writings of Yiddish authors and poets are being translated into various languages, including English, and have received their due recognition by literary critics. There is absolutely no reason to be ashamed of or to hide the Yiddish newspaper.

1939

Worthy Editor,

I have a neighbor who has been my good friend for over ten years, whose son is the hero of the story I'm writing you here. The son is now twenty-five, but I've known him since his childhood.

The young man finished public school and didn't want to study further. He got involved in sports, in playing baseball, in boxing, then wanted to become a prize fighter. I wonder why he didn't, because he has the strength of an ox. But he became a truck driver and earns good wages. He is a good-natured fellow and respects his parents.

My neighbor's son was brought up in a Jewish neighborhood, but he always went with Gentile friends and married an Irish girl. His parents, freethinking people, did not hinder him. If they had been against the match, most likely he would not have listened. He was never interested in *Yiddishkeit* so he settled with his wife, with whom he leads a fine home life, in a neighborhood where there are no Jews. Since his family name sounds American, probably the neighbors don't even know they have a Jew among them.

Lately I had occasion to ride in the subway with my neighbor's son. When we got into the car I noticed there was only one man there. He stood with his back to us and I saw that he was drawing on the wall with black crayon. He drew a swastika and under the hooked cross in heavy black letters he wrote, "Death to the Jews. Choke them wherever you meet them. Heil Hitler." He was so wrapped up in his work, he didn't even hear us come into the empty car.

My companion didn't say a word but went up to the man and before he could turn around punched him in the ear and then the nose. The man fell unconscious. We went into another car and got off the subway at the next station.

My friend's son soon took another subway, and I remained on the platform and watched from a distance as they led out the bleeding man, who couldn't stand on his feet. An ambulance doctor soon came, washed away the blood from his swollen face, and bandaged the wounds.

When I got home and told my wife about the incident, she said that my neighbor's son should not have beaten up the Nazi. She felt we should have held him and called a policeman to arrest him and he would have been punished. What is your opinion? We want to hear what you have to say about it.

> Respectfully,
> A Reader and his Wife

ANSWER:

We agree with the woman. It would have been proper for the writer and his companion to have the Nazi arrested, so he would have been penalized for defacing the walls of a public place, and for writing words that are simply an incitement to murder. He would not have been able to deny it, because they had caught him red-handed. Newspapers would have written about it and it could have served as a warning to other Nazi hooligans.

1941

Dear Editor,

My husband and I came from Galicia to America thirty-three years ago right after we were married. At home I had received a secular education, and my husband had been ordained as a rabbi. However, he did not want to be a rabbi here, and since we had brought along a little money from home, we bought a small business and made a good living. My husband is religious but not a fanatic. I am more liberal, but I go to *shul* with him on *Rosh Hashanah* and *Yom Kippur*.

We have five children—two boys and three girls. The boys went to a *Talmud Torah*, and the girls, too, received a Jewish education. We always kept a Jewish home and a *kosher* kitchen.

Our eldest son is now a college teacher, tutors students privately, and earns a good deal of money. He is married, has two children, four and seven years old. They live in a fine neighborhood, and we visit them often.

It happened that on Christmas Eve we were invited to have dinner with friends who live near our son and daughter-in-law, so we decided to drop in to see them after the meal. I called up, my daughter-in-law answered the telephone and warmly invited us to come over.

When we opened the door and went into the living room we saw a large Christmas tree which my son was busy trimming with the help of his two children. When my husband saw this he turned white. The two grandchildren greeted us with a "Merry Christmas" and were delighted to see us. I wanted to take off my coat, but my husband gave me a signal that we were leaving immediately.

Well, I had to leave at once. Our son's and daughter-in-law's pleading and talking didn't help, because my husband didn't want to stay there another minute. He is so angry at our son over the Christmas tree that he doesn't want to cross the threshold of their home again. My son justifies himself by saying he takes the tree in for the sake of his children, so they won't feel any different than their non-Jewish friends in the nighborhood. He assures us that it has nothing to do with religion. He doesn't consider it wrong, and he feels his father has no right to be angry over it.

My husband is a *kohen* and, besides having a temper, he is stubborn, too. But I don't want him to be angry at our son. Therefore I would like to hear your opinion on this matter.

With great respect,
A Reader from the Bronx

ANSWER:

The national American holidays are celebrated here with love and joy, by Jews and Gentiles alike. But Christmas is the most religious Christian holiday and Jews have nothing to do with it. Jews, religious or not, should respect the Christmas holiday, but to celebrate it would be like dancing at a stranger's wedding. It is natural that a Jew who observes all the Jewish traditions should be opposed to seeing his son and grandchildren trimming a Christmas tree.

But he must not quarrel with his son. It is actually your husband's fault because he probably did not instill the Jewish traditions in his son. Instead of being angry with him, he should talk to his son and explain the meaning of Christmas to him.

1943

Dear Editor,

As you see, this letter comes to you from a Western city, where I have been living for thirty-odd years. I am socially active here in the local Jewish community and belong to an Orthodox *shul* where I am recording secretary. Our rabbi here is from the old country and delivers his sermons in Yiddish because he is not fluent in the English language.

Not long ago, when we were holding an executive meeting in the rabbi's house, which is in an added wing built on the *shul*, someone phoned, and since I was sitting near the telephone, I answered. To my surprise, it was an acquaintance of mine, a man with an Irish name, who runs a large pork market. He told me he wanted to see our rabbi. I wondered what kind of business such a man could have with our rabbi, but I made an appointment for him. I also offered to be the interpreter at the meeeting, because I knew it would be hard for the rabbi to converse with him in English. But he answered that he wanted a private talk with the rabbi and would manage to make himself understood.

I want to remark here that this Irishman was well known in the city, not only for his large pork business but also because he played a big part in politics. He is a man in his late sixties, six feet tall, straight as a yardstick, and looks a lot younger than his age. He knows everybody and is friendly with all. He has two daughters, already married. And two years ago he became a widower.

The next day I came to the rabbi to find out about the meeting. He told me that the man, whom everybody considered an Irishman, wanted to become a member in our *shul*, and that he didn't have to convert because he is a Jew. He told the rabbi he had come to America as a youth from a small town in the same area the rabbi came from, and had even known his family. Here, he had shortened his name so it sounded Gentile, and later married a Christian girl who didn't know he was Jewish.

After their marriage, when his wife complained that he avoided going to church with her, he told her he was Jewish. She didn't tell anyone about it and it remained a secret. In time he became wealthy and well known in the city.

When Hitler came to power and began his reign of terror,

his Jewishness was awakened and he began to donate money to Jewish institutions and to help the unfortunate Jews in Europe. But he did it anonymously and no one knew where the money came from. At that time he wanted to avow his Jewishness openly, but his wife begged him not to, for the sake of their daughters.

After his wife's death he finally decided to take the step. Now the situation is this: the rabbi is willing to take him in as a member in our *shul*, but he demands that the man give up his pork market. The man is reluctant to do it but is ready to hand the business over to his two sons-in-law. The rabbi argues that as long as he has an income from the business he cannot become a member of the *shul*. This opinion is shared by most of the congregation. I think, however, that we are not treating him fairly: whatever his business, we should take him in as a member in our *shul*.

In our city we also have a fine Reform Temple and I told the man he should join it. But he wants to belong to our Orthodox *shul*, which he also wants to endow liberally.

We would like very much to hear your opinion, whether our rabbi has the right to act this way, and whether we should not allow this man to join our *shul*.

> Respectfully,
> The Recording Secretary

ANSWER:

An outsider cannot judge this problem. This is a purely religious matter and must be judged by the rabbi. Your rabbi surely knows that the *Talmud* says, "If a man wants to cleanse himself from sin, you must help him." We are sure the rabbi wants to help this man, but at the same time he must follow the Jewish law.

Regarding the rabbi's judgment, a reader from Manchester, New Hampshire, wrote the following letter:

Worthy Editor,

With all due respect for the unknown rabbi, I must say that his answer to the man who wants to return to Judaism disappointed me. I even doubt that his decision is in agreement with Jewish law.

When a Gentile wants to become a Jew he is confronted with certain difficulties. This is done to make sure he really means it sincerely and won't change his mind later about being a Jew. But when a lost Jew wants to find his way back to his people, it is our duty to help him and accept him with open arms.

This is not the only case where a Jew, because of various circumstances, lives among Gentiles, intermarries and becomes one of them. We have lost many Jews this way. And when it happens that such a Jew wants wholeheartedly to return to his religion, he must be given every opportunity. It is written, "A Jew, even when he has sinned, is still a Jew."

For the rabbi to demand that the man give up his pork market is a little too much to ask. One of the reasons why a Jew may not deal in pork is that he might be tempted to eat it himself. That is the law. But what happens to the law when in almost every community, especially in the suburbs, most of the *shul* members are not very careful when it comes to *kashruth* and eat non-*kosher* foods openly at various places?

We know that if every member, on joining a congregation, were ordered to eat only *kosher* foods, many *shuls* wouldn't have a *minyan*. The rabbi certainly knows that the sin of desecrating the Sabbath publicly is greater than dealing with pork. Does every *shul* member then avoid desecrating the Sabbath?

In general, it is hard to apply all Orthodox laws to *shul* members in America. In more than one congregation, they thank God that a Jew comes to *shul* once in a while and donates money to keep it up. Therefore I think that demanding that a man give up his business and ruin himself financially in order to become a member of the *shul* at a time when other *shul* leaders are desecrating the Sabbath is not just.

My opinion is that the man should be accepted as a member of the *shul*, without conditions. When he comes to the *shul*, the rabbi will then be able to see how sincere he is, whether he is a desirable member or not.

Respectfully,
H.S.

1943

Worthy Editor,

I write to you here about a vital question and wait impatiently for your opinion.

I came to America as a young girl, thirty-three years ago. My uncle, who brought me over, took me into the shop where he worked. And there I met a boy, also a "greenhorn." We fell in love and were married four months later.

I worked along with my husband till I was well along in my pregnancy. I gave birth to a boy. Three years later I had another boy, and then in another three, a girl. We cared for our children and strove to give them the best of everything. In time my husband took over a small store and I, as well as the children when they grew up, helped him. We worked hard to make a living, and we were happy with our children, who were studious and obedient. Even when they went to college they helped us in the store.

You can't imagine our joy when our eldest son graduated as a doctor. By that time our second son was already going to college and our daughter attending high school. Our son, the doctor, could have married a girl with a large dowry. Instead he married a fine girl, also a college graduate, whose parents are not wealthy, but decent people. The couple is very much in love, they have a darling little son, and have lived happily.

When Hitler began the war, our eldest son decided to volunteer for the army. Our children were always interested in world affairs and were concerned with the Jewish problems. I tried to talk him out of it, and told my husband to discourage him but my husband told me that our son knew what he was doing.

I ran to my daughter-in-law, because I thought she, too, didn't want him to leave her alone with the child, and to give up the practice he had worked up. Yet she began to console me and held back her tears. In short, my doctor went.

Then we, that is, America, declared war and our second son also enlisted in the army. That time I didn't raise a fuss, because I knew they would draft him anyway.

My heart is breaking, but I know I am not the only mother whose sons went to war. I know they must fight now for our dear country and we must make sacrifices to destroy our enemies. If it were not enough that our sons went away, now our daughter wants to join the WACs. When she told me this, it was as if I were struck on the head with a club.

I worry about her. She is not yet married. All the young men are in the army and now she wants to enlist in the army like her brothers. Instead of discouraging her, my husband says that if he were younger he wouldn't stay home either.

I am a simple woman. I understand clearly that a terrible wrath is being poured out on our world, and that we Jews should be more interested than all others in overcoming the bitter enemy. But must I, with my two sons in the war, also give up my daughter?

Many times I read the "Bintel Brief" to my daughter. She thinks highly of your wise answers, and agrees to wait until you print my letter and state your opinion.

With thanks,
An Unhappy Mother

ANSWER:

We understand fully how you feel. The fact is that we are all patriotic and loyal to our country, and we simply cannot talk your daughter out of serving in the women's military corps. She will get along well there, and when she comes back home you will very likely be pleased that she will have learned a great deal from her experience.

Naturally, a mother hopes for a good future for her daughter. But it is possible that the good future can come from her service in the WACs.

1944

Worthy Editor,

My husband is serving in the navy, and since he was always a reader of the *Forverts*, I still send him the paper regularly. It certainly will not be a surprise to him to read this letter that I beg you to print, because he knows about our problem.

I'll make it as short as possible. We have two sons, nine and seven years old. They are healthy, well built, and are doing well in public school and Hebrew school. So you would think everything is fine, but I have trouble with the older boy.

About nine months ago he took it into his head to become a vegetarian and stopped eating meat. At first I thought he was tired of meat and in time would forget his vegetarianism. For a few weeks I gave him other foods, then served him meat again, but he didn't touch it. Not only that, but as soon as he smelled meat cooking he wouldn't come into the kitchen.

My husband was still home at the time, and we took our son to a doctor who examined him and told us he was all right. He told us to have patience with the boy and in time he would start eating meat again. But there is no end to it.

He is stubborn. Not only does he refuse meat, but he doesn't even eat fish or sardines. He refuses to eat anything that was once alive.

Worthy Editor, advise me what to do. I'm afraid my son will grow up to be sickly if he doesn't eat meat. When my husband was home, we took him to a restaurant so he could see that everyone eats meat, and we hoped it would awaken his appetite for meat dishes. But it didn't help. What can we do?

>With thanks for your answer,
>The Worried Mother

ANSWER:

In the answer, the mother is advised to find out where her son got the idea to become a vegetarian, and then, with the help of a specialist, she might be able to bring him back to eating meat and fish. She is calmed and assured that a good doctor would know how to treat her nine-year-old vegetarian and in time her son would begin to eat meat again.

A few weeks later the *Forward* printed a reply to the answer, from the secretary of the Jewish Vegetarians Society in New York, that read as follows:

Dear Editor,

A short time ago your newspaper printed a letter from a mother who complained about her "great misfortune" that her nine-year-old son had become a vegetarian. The mother asked you for advice, and we wonder why you did not recommend that she contact us. Instead of introducing her to the large family of vegetarians here in New York, you advised her to take the boy to a doctor who would find a way to induce him to eat meat again.

As a vegetarian for thirty years, who has raised three children as vegetarians, in the best of health, I want to tell this mother that her fear of vegetarianism is groundless. On the contrary, it is important that young children should eat less meat. I know doctors who say that children up to the age of six do not need meat.

Not only in America, but all over the world, there are many vegetarians who bring up their children this way. Especially in England, now that there is food rationing because of the war, vegetarianism is widespread. The British Food Minister has on many occasions praised the vegetarians' diet and advised the masses to use it.

1945

Dear Editor,

Not long ago, through the *Forverts*, I learned that my brother's eight-year-old child was alive and living in France with a Gentile family. They are fine people, but I do not want my brother's child to remain with the Gentiles.

I had hoped my brother and his wife would survive the concentration camps where they were dragged by the German beasts three years ago, but there is no trace of them. I also had another brother with a wife and children in Poland, but so far I have heard nothing from them either. You can imagine how I feel and what is going on in my heart.

Now I want to rescue at least this one child for our people, and I ask your advice about it.

I often send packages for the child; I deny myself and do all I can, but it is not enough. My heart aches that my brother's child was converted and is being raised by Christians. I want to bring the child to America. I'm prepared to sign papers that I will keep it as my own. But my family try to talk me out of it.

The fact is that the family in France that is raising the child doesn't want to give it up, because they love him very much. They tell me it will be hard to do anything, and that

I must get a French lawyer because it will have to be fought in court. But I can't undertake it alone, and there's no one to help me. I have married daughters, and they think it would be better for the child to leave it where it is.

I am not a religious woman, but I am a Jewish daughter and I want the children of my family to remain Jewish. What shall I do? Where shall I go? I'm willing to fight to get the child and bring it to me. Help me save this Jewish child from growing estranged. I will thank you forever.

Respectfully,
Your Reader, H.Z.

ANSWER:

The writer of this letter is advised not to let herself be put off by those who say it's difficult to do anything in this matter. It is suggested that she should go to HIAS (Hebrew Immigrant Aid Society), not to give up going to the various organizations, to knock on many doors and write letters to special offices. She is given hope that somehow she will be able to get the child away from the Gentile family.

1952

Worthy Friend Editor,

I am a new immigrant and I have been in the city from which I write this letter for two years. I had a big family in Poland, and they were all murdered by the Hitlerites and their accomplices. I managed to escape to Russia, and so kept alive.

Now you can imagine what I felt and experienced when I recently met, here, the murderer of my sister, brother-in-law and their nine-year-old daughter.

My brother-in-law had been very wealthy and had a beautiful home in Poland with fine paintings and antiques. When the Germans seized Poland he left his home and possessions in the hands of a Pole who had worked for him a long time, and he and his family fled to a city which at that time was in Russian hands. When that city, too, was overrun by the Germans, they returned to their home and a good Pole gave them a place to hide. He wouldn't even take money for this.

My brother-in law took, with him to his hiding place only his antiques and valuable possessions. But a few weeks later his former employee, with whom he had left everything else, came to tell him that, if he didn't replace all the things he had taken out of the house, he would turn him over to the Germans. Good friends of my brother-in-law advised him to give the Pole everything, and so he did. The murderous Pole who had worked for my brother-in-law soon came again. That time he demanded that my brother-in-law sign a paper saying that he had sold him the house and all the precious things for fifteen thousand dollars. Again his friends advised him to give in to the Pole and he signed the paper.

A week later his former employee came with five Polish policemen and two Germans to my brother-in law in his hiding place. They took him, my sister and their child, as well as the good man who was hiding them, led them away to a small woods, and the murderous Pole himself shot them all. People who lived near the woods told all about it.

When I went back home after the holocaust, a brother and sister of the good Pole who had been shot along with my family told me everything. I went with them, then, to the Polish police chief, who was a decent man, and asked him why the murderer and robber who had worked with the Germans was still free. He answered with tears in his eyes that not he but a Russian commandant had all the authority.

I went to the Russian commandant with the same question, and his answer was that the time had not yet come to do anything about it. But it turned out that they arrested the brother and sister of the murdered Pole, and then came looking for me. I found out later that the man who had killed my sister, her husband and child now worked for the Russian secret police. I saw what was going on, what kind of justice I could expect, and I was afraid to stay there any longer. I could not bear watching that murderer living in my sister's house, going about free, so I left Europe.

But fate willed that I meet the murderer of my sister and her family. After being in this country awhile, I went to a wrestling match—and there I saw him. The moment I recognized him, I almost went crazy and wanted to take revenge immediately. However, the thought that I have a wife and young child who would suffer because of it kept me from doing it.

Since the murderer did not know me, I began a conversation with him, after I calmed down a little, and so in a roundabout way found out where he lives, whether he is already a citizen, and other things. I have since met him again at a football game.

I beg you to print this letter, and maybe people who could be witnesses at a trial will respond. At the same time I ask you to advise me how to act in this matter. I wait impatiently for your answer.

Respectfully,
A.G.

ANSWER:

We were very stirred by your letter and we feel with you in your pain and anxiety. It is good that you had the strength to control yourself when you met the murderer of your sister and her family and that you did not take revenge yourself. But this must not be kept quiet, and this murderer must absolutely be brought to trial.

But first you must consult representatives of Jewish organizations in your city about this. We hope that among our many readers there will be found survivors from that vicinity [name of the city was printed in the letter] who will come forth and testify to the accusations against the murderer.

1952

Dear Editor,

The question came up in our family as to how religious parents who keep strictly *kosher* should act when they come to visit their children who do not keep *kosher* homes. Should religious people eat non-*kosher* meat when they are at their children's homes in order not to insult them?

My opinion is that non-religious children respect their religious parents more when they live up to their beliefs and don't eat non-*kosher* foods. Others in the family do not agree with me.

I say that in America, where, thank God, there is enough food, everyone can indulge himself with whatever food he desires. And when children know that their parents keep a *kosher* home, they should not even think of serving them non-*kosher* meat.

The parents do not visit that often, and the children should not find it difficult to make a dinner that they know is *kosher* and can eat. They should do this out of respect for their parents. But not everybody in the family agrees with me. Therefore I decided to write to you for your opinion. The fact is that parents are concerned because they think their children will be insulted if they don't eat the food they prepare.

With respect and thanks,
M.A.

ANSWER:
We cannot imagine that children would demand of their religious parents that they eat their non-*kosher* food. In such a case, the parents do not have to adapt to the children's way, but just the opposite. Not the children but the parents should feel insulted when they come to visit and are served a non-*kosher* meal.

1953

Worthy Mr. Editor,

I write you this letter for the sake of my parents, who are readers of your newspaper, and because I know that they will accept your opinion. I have to write in English, because my Yiddish is not too good.

My problem is not a new one. I am a young man, American born, raised by religious parents who emigrated from Europe. During the past few years I went out with nice, attractive Jewish girls, but I fell in love with none of them. I waited for my true love, but as if for spite, the girl is not Jewish. I went out with this girl once and we fell in love.

This Gentile girl is refined, has a good character and many fine qualities. I could write a lot about her, but what good would it do? You yourself know what words can be used by someone deeply in love.

I expected that my religious parents would oppose my marrying a non-Jewish girl, but I can't understand their attitude. If they told me they didn't want to see me again, or have anything to do with me, it would hurt me, because I love my parents. But I would still have hope that in time they would forgive me and we would be close again. But when I told them about the girl they warned me that if I married her they would commit suicide. And knowing my parents, I'm afraid. They say that it would be a terrible shame and heartache and they would have nothing to live for any more.

Worthy Editor, I know that many mixed marriages are unhappy, but I feel I will be happy with this girl. Therefore I ask you to explain to my parents that they must rid themselves of these thoughts and stop talking about suicide, even though they are very grieved. I am very disturbed by their talk. This girl is as dear to me as life itself and I don't know what to do.

Thank you very much for your answer,

Respectfully,
D.F.

ANSWER:
We are of the opinion that you should not marry the non-Jewish girl. You should break off the match not only for the sake of your parents but for your own too, because you are from two different worlds. Even if your parents stopped talking about suicide, you would become a stranger to them and the whole family forever.

Since you were raised in a religious home, you would not be able to live harmoniously with a Gentile wife and would feel like a stranger in her family. Love alone cannot fill a life. Consider this matter thoroughly before it is too late.

1954

Worthy Editor,

Since I don't want to take up too much of your time and space, I'll come right to the point and ask your advice.

In the town where I live there is a Jewish Center where young and old gather. They also go there to pray on the Sabbath and holidays. But a few years ago they raised the price of a ticket for *Rosh Hashanah* and *Yom Kippur* so much that quite a number of people couldn't or wouldn't pay. At that time we got together and founded an Orthodox *shul,* which our town had never had until that time.

Naturally it was not as comfortable in our little *shul* as

it had been in the large Center. Also the membership is not as large and it is not easy to maintain the *shul* and our Orthodox rabbi.

I derive great pleasure worshiping in our *shul* in the old-time Orthodox manner; however, my dear wife is not satisfied. She prefers the modern Center. She argues that at the Center the men and women sit together, and when I sat next to her I could always point out which prayers we were saying. In my Orthodox *shul* she must sit among the women. She also complains that I am too involved and it costs me too much to support the *shul*. She thinks there is no future for the *shul* in our town because during the week it is hard to gather even the ten men for a *minyan*.

As I said, I love the *shul* and it's a pleasure to work to support it and the rabbi, who has a family of small children, may they all be well. If I were to leave the *shul* it might go under altogether. I don't know what to do. Therefore I decided to write you about it and I thank you in advance for your answer.

With friendly regards,
A *Shul* Member

ANSWER:

Your wife should have talked this problem over with you before you threw yourself into the work of founding an Orthodox *shul* in your town. She should have told you previously that she preferred worshiping in the Center, where men and women sit together. Now that you have the *shul* that you helped establish, now that she sees you deriving such pleasure praying there, she must not demand that you go back to the Center.

1955

Worthy Friend Editor,

My wife and I work very hard in our candy store, which is open seven days a week and sixteen hours a day. We make a living, and during the past fifteen years we've been in business, we've saved enough money to buy ourselves a small house.

Two years ago my daughter, who is now finishing her studies to become a nurse, bought me an art kit for my birthday, a box with pencils and various paints that artists use. She gave me the present because she knows that I used to like drawing and painting over twenty years ago. She told me I should try to paint again, but not to copy other pictures. Since I am a little nervous, my daughter thought that this would calm my nerves.

I was overjoyed with the gift, and in the limited time when I could tear myself away from the store, I began to paint and draw from nature and from life. I also managed to go to an art school for a week, and it's impossible to describe my pleasure. I painted a lot during these two years and some of my pictures have been accepted for exhibitions. There was even a write-up about me in an English newspaper.

I set up my "studio" for working in the basement between the cases of seltzer, boxes of candy and other things. I paint late at night too, after we close the store.

Not long ago a rich businessman, from whom I buy merchandise for the store, saw a picture of mine, and since he liked it, he invited me to his luxurious home to show me his artistic wall paintings, called murals. He asked me if I would be able to paint such murals, and I must confess to you that I almost cried, because I was sure that I could. They seemed like nothing compared to my paintings. I later showed the businessman some wall paintings I had made for a neighbor of mine, and now he wants me to paint several murals in his home. He tells me I would be able to make a living painting murals.

My wife, daughter and friends, too, think I should begin to devote myself to painting only, and I want to hear your opinion of this. Painting is my whole life, but I am already forty-nine years of age, and perhaps it's too late for one to become a professional painter of murals.

                    With thanks for your answer,
                    L.L.

ANSWER:

You are still far from being old, and it is never too late to accomplish something. We could list names here of many people who, in their late years, achieved a great deal in various fields and became famous. Meanwhile, however, you should not give up the store. It would be good, though, if you could hire someone to help you in the business, so that you could devote more time to painting. You must not give up the painting that gives meaning to your life and brings you so much pleasure. This is, for you, a newly discovered treasure that is priceless.

1955

Worthy Friend Editor,

My husband and I have been happily married for six years. This is a second marriage, for both of us and we each have children, all of them now independent.

I now have a problem facing me, and I beg you earnestly to give me advice through the "Bintel Brief."

When my husband's first wife died, he was very grieved and had a double headstone placed on her grave, because he didn't think he would marry again. As time passed, however, and his wound began to heal, he realized it is not good to remain alone. After that, the following occurred:

My present husband and I are *landsleit* and have been good friends since our youth. We also belong to the same society and we often met at the meetings. When he lost his wife I was already a widow, and as time went on we poured out our loneliness to each other and he suggested that we should marry.

I accepted his suggestion, and we were married. We adjusted well and are both happy.

At times we have occasion to go to the cemetery of our *landsleit*, where my first husband, my brother, relatives and my present husband's first wife are buried. Every time I pass her grave and see the double headstone with his name, I feel so bad that I get sick.

This is always on my mind, because I would like my husband to lie near me after the hundred and twenty years, and our graves should not be far apart. So I ask you to advise me what can be done about it.

> With thanks and respect,
> A.D.

ANSWER:

Since you and your husband belong to the same society, you must have known about the double headstone before you married him, and if you said nothing to him about it then, you must now make no demands of him. You must understand it is no minor task for your husband to remove the headstone from the double grave. Just for the sake of his children and the members of the society, it is difficult for him to do this.

You married your second husband, not to have a piece of ground together, but because you wanted a friend in life, and since you have achieved that, you should be satisfied. Why should you destroy your happiness with thoughts of what will happen in the future?

1955

Dear Editor,

I am already a grandmother with grown-up grandchildren, may they be well, but I have not yet forgotten my anxiety when my own children were growing up and not yet married.

I came from Europe with young children, sons and daughters, and before I could look around, boys began calling on my girls. And when my daughters began to go out with the boys, I used to worry and run to the window to see if they were coming home yet. My husband would tell me I should trust our daughters, and the boys who came to them as well, but I used to think, "Who knows what they are doing?"

Now, in my later years, I live with one of my daughters, and I practically run the house, since she and her husband are in business all day. The daughter I live with has a girl not quite sixteen, who's already going out with a boy of the same age. And now when I see them together I worry just as I used to when her mother was still single.

When my granddaughter and the boy walk from school, they hold hands, they kiss, and spend a lot of time alone at home. My daughter and son-in-law know he comes to the house—or better, never leaves the house—and they don't mind. But I worry and I'm afraid to leave them alone. They tell me they love me, but they'd love me more if I weren't watching them so much.

I don't know whether I should talk to my daughter or whether I should see, hear and keep quiet. But I can't stand watching how two young children behave. They are too young to understand that such free behavior could have bad results. It seems the only thing to do is get them married. Yet they are only children.

I would like to hear your advice.

With thanks,
A Grandmother

ANSWER:

It's true that today's youth behave more freely than those of a few generations ago. Most educators of our era believe, too, that children should be reared with a great deal of freedom. It should, however, be within certain limits. We say this in reference to your grandaughter, who has been given a little too much freedom.

If there really is cause for worry about your granddaughter's behavior, you must absolutely talk to your daughter about it. She must find the time to pay more attention to her daughter. Your granddaughter needs her mother's companionship now more than ever.

1956

Worthy Mr. Editor,

When I read the "Bintel Brief" in the *Forverts* it reminded me of how they used to run to the *rebbe* in Poland with all kinds of problems. And now, to come to the point about my problem:

Years have gone by since the sharp fangs of the mad beast destroyed a third of the Jewish people. Thanks to the Allied armies, the beasts in human form were defeated, but with those who were saved by a miracle the nightmares and aftereffects of the destruction remain.

When the living, the lucky ones, began to come out of their hiding places and regained a bit of their normalcy, they began to rebuild their shattered lives. So it was with me and my present wife. The murderers killed my first wife and our two children, and my present wife lost her husband and a child. When we met, we decided to marry, establish a home, and start to build a new life, since this was the thing to do.

Now we are here in America, we already have two children, may they be well, who are eight years old, and my wife and I often discuss whether we should tell them about the tragic past. I mean, about our personal losses, because I have told them about the general destruction. I feel we should not tell them yet about the loss of our own children, but wait until they are older. My wife, however, thinks the opposite, and sometimes she comes out with a half statement and the children are disturbed.

Now I ask you, who is right, I or my wife? Should the children be told everything now, or is there time yet? I believe you will give us the right answer.

Respectfully,
H.S.
Brooklyn

ANSWER:

Certainly we should tell our children about the holocaust, about the horrible massacres that the German murderers and those who helped them perpetrated on our people, and about the fact that the whole world was silent. Certainly we must see to it that the future generations know and remember what the German Amalek did to the Jews. But we agree with you that your little children, who are a great comfort to you after all your sufferings, do not need to be burdened yet with the anxiety and sorrow. It would be advisable for you and your wife to let it go until later, when they will be better able to understand the tragic history of the annihilation of the six million Jews.

1956

Worthy Mr. Editor,

I am an old reader of yours and I come to you for advice in our situation.

Our son served in the American air force and spent a lot of time in England. There he fell in love with a Gentile girl and wrote me and my wife that we should give him our consent to marry her. But we were against the marriage, and I tried in every letter to point out to him that most mixed marriages are not successful.

In time we also got a letter from his girl friend, who wrote that she loved our son very much and was willing to convert to the Jewish religion. I answered her, explained how difficult it is to be a Jew, pointed out the problems and troubles the Jews have encountered in various eras in Spain, Russia, Germany and other countries. She replied that she knew all about that, but that she likes the Jewish religion, is ready to convert, and hopes to raise her children as Jews.

My wife and I didn't know what to do and I went to the office of the Orthodox rabbis. I told the story to a board of four rabbis and they said that we should give our consent.

In brief, the couple was married. A short time ago they came to America with their child and we took them into our home. The daughter-in-law converted to Judaisim and observes the Jewish laws. She lights the Sabbath candles, *koshers* the meat and keeps meat and dairy dishes separate. She is a fine, intelligent woman and we make every effort to draw her closer to us. She has no parents, only a grandmother and grandfather in England, who had also been against the marriage and are therefore estranged from her.

Our son had a good Jewish upbringing, he reads and writes Yiddish, he knows Jewish history and when he was in England he corresponded with his grandmother in Yiddish. My mother, who is over eighty already, is a well-educated woman and she keeps up with everything going on in the world. No one of us can stump her on politics. But she was very much against the match, and when my son, on his return from England, called her on the phone, she told him that she didn't want to see him. I have spoken with her several times about it, but it doesn't help.

Now we have a problem. My brother is making a wedding for his daughter and we are all invited. My son is in a quandry. Should he introduce his wife to his grandmother at the wedding? What is your opinion? I ask you to answer soon.

> With thanks and respect,
> A Worried Father

ANSWER:

We think that at the wedding, where the whole family will be together, it would be a good opportunity for your son to make up with his grandmother and introduce his wife to her. But first someone from the family should speak to the grandmother to prepare her for it.

If your aged mother is an educated, understanding woman, she should realize it's high time to make peace with her grandson and draw closer to his wife, who is now a Jewish daughter and part of the family.

1956

Dear Friend Editor,

I was sitting with a group of old friends who were speaking nostalgically about the "good old days," and I interrupted with the question, Were the old days really that good? In connection with the discussion we had, we would like to hear your opinion.

I think that when older people long for the old days and say it was better then, it's only because they were young and still had their whole lives before them. But the truth is that those times were not so good.

I still remember my home town in Russia, our simple little house lighted at night by a small kerosene lamp, the door thatched with straw nailed down with sackcloth to keep it warm in winter. I still remember the mud in the streets of the town, so deep it was difficult to get around; our fear of the Gentiles; and who can forget the poverty—the times when there wasn't even a crust of bread?

When we came to New York, I thought we were entering heaven. But here in the new land, in those old days, we lived on the East Side in tenements and had to climb to the fourth and fifth floors to tiny rooms that were dark and airless. There were no bathrooms in the flats. A large bathtub stood in the kitchen near the old iron stove that was heated with coal in which mothers also did the laundry.

In those "good days" we worked in the shops fourteen and sixteen hours a day, six days a week, and the bosses treated the workers like slaves. Summertime, in the great heat, we couldn't breathe in the house at night and we slept on the roofs or on the sidewalks.

When I think of the modern conveniences we live with now, of the wonderful inventions, achievements in various fields, that we enjoy, and about the opportunities for everyone in this blessed country, I see there's nothing to be nostalgic about. I say we now have the good times and we do not have to long for the past.

Not all my friends agree with me, and it will be interesting for us to hear what you have to say about it.

> With great respect,
> K.S.

ANSWER:

Your conclusion is correct. The little town with its mud, the poor hut with the kerosene lamp, the bitter life in Czarist Russia and the old-time sweatshops here, contrast dramatically with to-day's comfortable life in our country. It's like the difference between day and night.

But it is natural for the older immigrant to see that past in beautiful colors. His longing is actually not for that time but for his childhood, his youth, when he was happy with very little.

1959

Worthy Editor,

I am a widower in my eighties, and the last few years, since I lost my wife, I wander from place to place. I've lived in several furnished rooms, spent a few weeks in an old-age home. Now I live in a hotel for the elderly but I am not happy.

I am a lonely man, though I have four children who are all very wealthy. They all have their own beautiful homes, but there is no place for me. It grieves me, but I can't do anything about it. There's no sense for me to tell you here what my wife and I did for our children and how they act toward me now. I am alone as if I had no one in the world. I know I am not the only one to find himself in such a state, but that is no comfort.

I am writing to you not about my loneliness, because nothing can be done about that. I want your advice about something else.

I am not dependent on my children and since I have several thousand dollars, I question what to do with my money. My children don't need my money and do not deserve any inheritance from me. Therefore I decided to leave all I have to a worthy cause. But I question whether I should leave everything to the State of Israel, which depends on the help of American Jewry, or to leave some for *yeshivas*, institutions and hospitals in the States.

I don't want to bequeath anything to my children, because they treat me badly. I hope you won't be offended that I bother you, and will answer me soon.

My thanks in advance,
A Devoted Reader

ANSWER:
In the answer to this man, it is emphasized that the young Jewish nation which opens its doors to Jews of all the world does need the support and should be helped as much as possible. But he must decide, himself, how to divide the inheritance. It is also explained that he must make a will and consult a lawyer about this matter.

1959

Worthy Editor,

Since I have been a faithful reader of the *Forverts* for the past forty years, I come to you for advice.

Briefly, this is the problem: For many years I have belonged to a Benevolent Society which is well known as an organization that provides burial for the poor who have no one to pay for the plot. Some time ago we bought ground for a cemetery and we still have room for about two hundred and forty graves. Lately, especially since older people have been receiving Social Security, they don't have to come to our society for help.

It's certainly good that people are now in better circumstances, but in our society the question has been raised about what to do now. We discussed selling about two hundred plots from our cemetery and sending the money to Israel. We, the members of our Benevolent Society, are no longer young and we must do something quickly. We know the money we will raise from the land will be useful in Israel.

We now question whether we should sell off the largest part of our ground, as we plan. Therefore we decided to ask you. We wait for your answer.

> Respectfully,
> One of the Members

ANSWER:

In order to be able to answer this question, we would have to be more familiar with the work of your organization and its constitution. We would also have to know how many plots you have given away to poor people lately. We find it unbelievable that it has reached the point where no one has to come to you for help.

But if everything is as you describe, it would be quite right to carry out your plan. In Israel there are still plenty of needy and your donation could do a great deal of good.

1960

Worthy Friend Editor,

People say a child should not be given in to, and this may be right. But I, a man in his sixties, married for thirty-three years, say that a wife should certainly not be given in to.

I don't want to speak ill of my dear wife, God forbid. On the contrary, she is faithful, a good housekeeper and a devoted mother, but a problem has arisen.

When television came into style, I bought one too, and my wife was very pleased. Both of us sat very often during the evenings watching the TV and enjoyed it. Since our children got married and left home, however, my wife began to spend all day at the TV.

A while ago she began to ask me to buy her a small TV set too, one that can be carried from one room to another, and for her birthday I bought her a portable TV set. And don't ask what happened. When we go to bed she puts the set in front of the bed and stays awake late into the night till she falls asleep.

I see now that I should not have given in to my wife, I should not have bought the TV set, because I bought myself trouble. I walk around half asleep and when I plead with my wife that she shouldn't keep the TV on so late she says that she never said a word when I used to read a newspaper or a book in bed. The truth is, though, that long ago I stopped reading in bed before going to sleep.

Now I ask myself: what did I need it for? And I write you this letter for the sake of other men, to let them know that even the best of wives shouldn't always be given in to. I hope that you, worthy Editor, have something to say about it.

With thanks and respect,
The Too Good Husband

ANSWER:

Whether you had to give in to your wife and buy her such a gift is your own business. But you should have discussed with her previously where and when she was to use the portable TV set. Keeping it on late into the night and not letting you sleep is a little too much.

There's no question that it's a good thing to have the "Wonder-Box" in the home, for millions and millions of people derive much enjoyment from it. But one should not allow oneself to spend too much time with TV. And certainly one should not keep it on late at night when one needs sleep. Even a "Too Good Husband" must not stand for it. Your wife must take this into consideration.

1961

Dear Friend Editor,

I am a workingman who struggled hard all these years to make a living for my wife and children. True, you can't get rich by working, but in the course of the years I have saved a little money. All these years I was satisfied and thanked God that I made a living.

Now I am ready to marry off a daughter, and the family want me to make the wedding at one of the finest hotels, with the best music, with many guests, as if I were a millionaire. I had planned to make a wedding that would cost about two thousand dollars, and that's more than enough for such a workingman as I.

My wife and daughter argue, though, that even poor people make big weddings today, because it's the style. This is true. I myself know people who borrow money to make fancy weddings, but to me this seems madness. A friend of mine is now deep in debt because he made a grandiose wedding for his daughter. The young couple have enough debts too. The young man didn't have a penny when he bought the engagement ring and he still has to pay and pay. And he bought furniture on installments too.

Now there are quarrels in my house about this, about what kind of wedding we should have. I can't convince my wife that we don't have to imitate others and that it is foolish to throw out hard-earned money just to show off for people. My wife is a faithful reader of the "Bintel Brief," and I therefore ask you to give your opinion on this matter.

With great respect,
A Troubled Father

ANSWER:
We, like you, think you must not play the role of a wealthy man when you are not one. People in your circumstances need not follow the style and must not make elaborate weddings. There's no sense to overextend yourself, drown yourself in debts, just to show off before *landsleit* and friends. It would be wiser to use some money to help the young couple get settled.

People in your class feel like masqueraders when they wear a tuxedo and top hat at these pompous affairs. For you and for your guests, a party arranged without show and fuss, but modest and homey, would be more to their liking.

1963

Dear Editor,

My husband and I had been readers of the *Forverts* even before we were married, and that's many years, since we are preparing to celebrate our golden wedding. Our children and grandchildren are making a big party for us and my husband wants to visit Israel to celebrate the occasion. But I question whether we should undertake such a long trip.

My husband has always been a Zionist. Even as a boy in Galicia he dreamed of going to Palestine. But his parents convinced him to go to his uncle in America, who wanted to send him a steamship ticket. And later, when he was here in the country, he still thought about going to Palestine. Meanwhile, over fifty years have passed.

When the State of Israel was established and our President Truman was the first to recognize it, my husband's desire to go to the Jewish homeland was reawakened. But he couldn't get away. At that time we already had two married daughters and grandchildren, my husband was involved with our sons in a big business, and we couldn't manage a trip, even for a few weeks.

We put it off from one year to the next, and when my husband gave up the business a year and a half ago, it was only after he had·had two heart attacks. Lately he feels fairly well, but I think it's too great a strain for him to make such a trip. He's in his late seventies and I'm trying to discourage him from making the journey.

My husband keeps saying he must see the Jewish homeland, and I also want to go. We want to see Israel and also our relatives there who escaped from the Nazi murderers. But I am afraid it would be too much for my husband.

We both want to hear your opinion and your advice and I beg you to answer quickly.

With thanks,
Mrs. G.S.

ANSWER:

It would certainly be a wonderful experience for your husband, as well as for you, to see the land of Israel and meet your relatives who found a home there. But it is not for us to judge whether your husband should undertake the trip. In such a case you must consult his doctor. Only the doctor can help you decide what to do.

1964

Dear Editor,

I am writing to you here about a family matter because it is very important for me to hear your opinion.

My husband and I have been married over forty years and we always got along well. We should say "God bless America" every day, because we always had a good family life and achieved a great deal. We raised three decent sons who are all professionals. They have been married a long time and we have a lot of pleasure from them and the grandchildren. One son lives near us and, though I am not very close to my daughter-in-law, we see them often.

But recently my daughter-in-law actually insulted me when I was in her house.

I came in when she and my son were talking about their son's *Bar Mitzvah*, which is to take place soon. They were planning when and where to have the dinner, and since my husband and I observe *kashruth*, I said the party should be held in a *kosher* place. My daughter-in-law turned up her nose and in an insulting tone told me they'd decide for themselves where and how to arrange the *Bar Mitzvah*. My son didn't say a word, and I left feeling very hurt.

A few weeks later our son telephoned my husband and let him know they decided on a strictly *kosher* place for the *Bar Mitzvah* party. But since my daughter-in-law insulted me, I have no great desire to go to the dinner. It would be enough for me to go to the *shul* on Saturday to see my grandson called up to the Torah and hear him chant the prayers.

My husband keeps telling me to ignore my daughter-in-law's words and says we should both go to the dinner. Must I go to the party? Please answer soon.

With thanks,
A Mother-in-Law

ANSWER:

It is obvious that you have a grudge against your daughter-in-law from before, and maybe you are justified. In spite of it, you must not be angry now. We don't know exactly what happened between you and her when you remarked that the dinner should be held at a *kosher* place. It is possible that she was not tactful in her answer to you, but that is not sufficient grounds for spoiling the party, which is yours too. This means you should listen to your husband and absolutely go with him to your grandson's *Bar Mitzvah*.

1965

Dear Editor,

I come to you about something that happened in the distant past, and I ask your advice.

Much could be written about those days when one was young, full of hopes and dreams. But I will make it short.

My husband and I have been together almost fifty years but we still look and feel younger than our age. We have children, grandchildren and even two great-grandchildren. I say "together" because that word involves a secret our children do not know. I had told this secret only to my brother many years ago. The secret is: my husband and I were never married legally. We never took out a marriage license, nor did we have a Jewish ceremony.

My husband and I were young immigrants when we got acquainted. I was not quite nineteen and my husband was a few months under twenty-one. We were members of an idealistic group who dreamed of building a heaven on earth for everyone. We believed in "free love."

My husband and I were alone here because our parents had remained in Europe. We fell deeply in love, and after a two weeks' friendship we decided to live together. We were not the only ones at that time to do so. It was the fashion, then, for "free love" among many liberal idealistic young men and women.

I can tell you that many young couples would hope to lead as beautiful a family life as we had. We lived in love and fidelity and the years flew by. But times and conditions brought change in our life. One could write a book about them. At one time my husband was a laborer and I was a shopgirl; but we have belonged for many years now to the "capitalist class." Our children are in the same position. Almost all of our grandchildren are professionals, one a leading scientist, another a rabbi. For many years we've been living in a fine house in a small town and—don't laugh—my husband is a good member of the synagogue here.

The fact that we never married legally, however, has been on our minds for many years—more than ever of late. This is because we are approaching our old age and our world is different. I tell my husband often, lately, that we should do something about it because we even feel guilty before our children. My husband thinks as I do about this, but he doesn't want to stir up the whole thing.

My brother lives in a city thousands of miles away, and since I haven't seen him in many years, I told my husband that we should go to visit him for a few weeks and there we could settle everything. I mean, get a marriage license and go to a rabbi to be married properly. We waited fifty years, and that's long enough. My husband is undecided and puts it off. I would, therefore, like to hear your point of view and your suggestion. I hope to read your reply soon in the "Bintel Brief."

A Grateful Reader

ANSWER:

We read your letter with keen interest and we came to the conclusion that the fact that the secret you have kept so many years torments you and doesn't let you rest is reason enough to do something about it. We cannot understand why you waited so long. You could have solved your problem, quietly, a long time ago so that no one would know about it.

Take this opportunity to visit your brother whom you haven't seen in a long time and there, in his city, go through the procedure of a legal and formal Jewish marriage. May that be a prelude to your fiftieth anniversary celebration of a happy and beautiful married life. The sooner you go through with this, the better it will be for you.

1965

Dear Editor,

We are three sisters, and as I am the oldest, it has fallen to me to write to you about our father, and to ask you earnestly to print this letter and your answer as soon as possible. Our parents are regular readers of the *Forward* and my husband, who is a rabbi, also reads your paper.

This is our problem. Our father is due to retire soon. He has worked hard many years in his small business, and Mama helped him. Even when we, their three children, were small, Mama ran to help Papa, who stayed in the store from early morning to late at night. Our father saved very little money in all these years. He has Social Security, his own little house and a little in the bank. He couldn't save because he didn't earn much and, in addition, he always had an open hand. He always liked to give to charity, more than he could afford.

The problem is that, now that he is planning to give up the store, he continues to carry on as before. He never refuses anyone who comes to him and asks for money for a worthy cause. His *landsleit* keep coming to him for advice and for help for the needy. Mama is more practical and she tells him they have to start living differently because their income will be smaller. Lately they're even beginning to quarrel about this, and we are all very upset.

My sisters and I agree with Mama, but we love our good father very much. His deepest pleasure is to help others, and we don't know what to do about it. Our whole family wants to hear your opinion on the question. Thank you in advance for your answer.

Respectfully,
Mrs. B.

ANSWER:

It is evident that your father is blessed with a fine character and a good nature. To help the needy and to give with an open hand to worthy causes is a virtue. One must always keep in mind, however, the need to keep oneself within bounds. Even in the name of charity, one must not give more than one can afford.

You must see to it, however, that your mother should not quarrel with your father because it is not easy to change a man of his years. You and your sisters must help your mother influence your father, now that he is retiring, to be more careful with the dollar, and to give only according to his means.

1966

Dear Editor,

I am writing you, with my dear husband's permission, about the resentment we feel over our daughter-in-law, and I ask your advice.

We have two daughters and a son. They and our grandchildren are very dear to us, and it is our greatest pleasure to visit with them. Lately, however, we have been very upset by our daughter-in-law and our son. We used to go to them, as to our daughters and sons-in-law, quite often, and used to spend a lot of time with their children, who are five and three years old.

Our daughter-in-law was never too friendly toward us, but we overlooked a great deal. A short time ago, when my husband and I went there, she suddenly announced that she wanted us to visit our grandchildren only once in two weeks, and that we should avoid coming to them on weekends when they have guests.

I didn't know at first what my daughter-in-law meant, but she explained that, as her children were growing up, she didn't want them to learn from us to speak English with a Jewish accent. Our dear daughter-in-law wasn't even ashamed to tell us that we didn't fit in with her group of friends who were real Americans, while we were foreigners.

It's true we're not American-born (we came to this country over forty years ago) and our English is not "perfect," but we are very hurt by our daughter-in-law's remark. I answered her then that in our youth we had no time to learn the English that was spoken in high society because we had to work hard to raise a college-educated husband for her. I told her my husband often had to work overtime in order to be able to send our son to college, to make him a professional man.

My husband didn't let me continue arguing with our daughter-in-law, who is a young, foolish girl, and we went home angry. The next day my son called up. I thought he would tell us his wife had been wrong, but he said that he agreed with her that we should visit them every other week on a definite day. Very distressed, I hung up in the middle of the conversation and my husband and I haven't visited them at all for the past few weeks.

We ask you, is this right? Should children act this way? What can we do, dear Editor, since we miss our grandchildren so? We are hurt and want to know whether we must obey these rules laid down by our daughter-in-law. Please answer soon.

> With heartfelt thanks,
> Grandma and Grandpa

ANSWER:

You are rightfully bitter. Your son should be blamed even more than your daughter-in-law. He should never have permitted her to make such an arrangement. It is also natural that you should feel offended by your daughter-in-law's statement. The behavior of your daughter-in-law is ridiculous and contrary to the American tradition. Many great men, active in American government, education and business, were brought up by immigrant parents who didn't speak English correctly, but this did not keep them from having successful careers. And these successful children of immigrants are not ashamed of their fathers and mothers who came to America from across the ocean. Just the opposite, they take every opportunity to mention their parents and grandparents with pride, and they stress the fact that these immigrants who speak English with a Jewish accent have enriched their lives.

We feel that someone in your family should explain this to your son and daughter-in-law, and they may see that they are wrong. We also feel that at present you should visit your grandchildren, your son and daughter-in-law, not as often as before, since a prolonged estrangement will do you more harm than them.

1967

Dear Editor,

I am the grandmother of a twenty-one-year-old girl, a girl with all the finest qualities, and I am writing to you about our problem with her.

Our granddaughter met a boy about six months ago, a boy a few years older than she. They fell in love and are already talking about marriage. The boy is very refined, from a good and wealthy family. He will be graduating from college this year and everything would be all right, if not for a "but."

Our son and daughter-in-law, the parents of the bride-to-be, belong to a Reform Temple and brought up their daughter in the same tradition. Her boy friend, however, comes from an Orthodox family who conform strictly to the Jewish code. In his home the phone is not answered on the Sabbath, and on Friday night the electricity is controlled by an automatic clock.

To our granddaughter all this was new and strange, but when

she fell in love with the boy and began visiting his home, she came to love his way of life. It has gone so far that she does not ride on Saturday or eat meat at her own home because she knows her mother does not keep a *kosher* kitchen, and she even wants to reform her parents.

Since my husband and I are not Orthodox either, she has been complaining to us too. She would like her boy friend to be able to eat in her home, and this means that she wants her mother to start keeping a *kosher* kitchen.

There are many quarrels about this, because my daughter-in-law won't hear of making such changes. She is generally indifferent to Judaism, and she would prefer to break up the match. The girl is considering moving out of her home, because she doesn't want to eat non-*kosher* food.

The question is how to handle the situation, and I ask you to answer immediately.

Watching for your answer,
Mrs. B.V.

ANSWER:

We feel that your granddaughter's boy friend's strict religious background need not be a hindrance to marriage. The main point is that he is a decent boy and that your granddaughter loves him. And her new belief in Orthodox Judaism should be considered a virtue, not a fault.

Your son, daughter-in-law and the entire family should not oppose the match. When your granddaughter marries the young man she'll be able to run her own home as she pleases, but she cannot and should not demand of her parents that they should change their way of life for her boy friend's sake. Your granddaughter and her parents, and even you, must restrain yourselves from giving each other advice on how to live. This is the time for tolerance, and you must all understand it.

1967

Worthy Editor,

My husband and I always got along well with both our sons, who have been married now for a long time, but I'm afraid we're heading for trouble in our family.

Our older son has a good government job and is quite satisfied. My husband took the younger son into the business when he was still quite young. When he got married my husband made him an equal partner.

My husband is not overambitious and satisfied with whatever the business brings in. But our son and even our daughter-in-law are complaining lately that they aren't making a living. They have two little children, they bought a house with a big mortage, they trade in the car every couple of years and they are always behind in their payments.

My son's main complaint is that his father doesn't let him enlarge and modernize the business. He's a young man, he wants to keep up with the times, and his father holds him back. My husband says the new innovations are just for spending money and, no matter what our son would do, the business wouldn't bring in any more money.

Lately our son goes around sulking and our daughter-in-law hints that he will have to look for a job to earn more money. But I would not want our son to leave his father alone now, in his declining years.

I am between two fires, because I think they're both right. The point is that my husband is near retirement age and I want my son to stay with him because he'll have to take over the whole business in time.

I would like to avoid a quarrel and beg you to give your opinion on this matter.

Many thanks,
Your Reader, Mrs. H.V.

ANSWER:
It is quite natural that your son, who is probably young and energetic, wants to keep up with the times. He has the ambition to modernize the business that is being run in an old-fashioned manner.

We are of the opinion that if your husband is near the age when he will be ready to turn the whole business over to his son he should now, little by little, give him a chance to show what he can do.

But if he is not yet thinking of retiring and is absolutely opposed to making changes in the business, then the son must not be hindered from looking for something else.

1967

Dear Editor,

I was born and raised in New York, of parents who have read the *Forward* all these years, and since I always spoke Yiddish at home and attended a Yiddish school, I can write this letter to you in Yiddish. Even as a young girl I read aloud for Mother and Grandma from the "Bintel Brief." In those days it never occurred to me that one day I would turn to you for advice.

I am twenty-seven years of age and the mother of a five-year-old. I have a dear, good husband and we enjoy a happy family life. A few years ago we bought a nice house in a good neighborhood and everything is fine as can be.

My problem will seem a little odd to you. I come to you to complain about my mother-in-law because she is too modern for me. In contrast with my mother-in-law, who is two years short of fifty, I'm an old-fashioned woman. When I disagree with her, she herself tells me we ought to change places.

A few years ago my mother-in-law lost her husband and she lived alone for a while. A few months ago, however, she fell ill and my husband talked her into giving up her home and moving in with us. She listened to him and I am not happy about it. My mother-in-law doesn't need our financial help—she has money and a good income, but since my husband is her only son, and she has no one else, she's happy to be living with us.

I love my husband; I love and respect my mother-in-law—but, don't laugh at me, we are from two opposite worlds. I like to stay home evenings, to read a book, sew or knit, listen to good music, and it's enough for me to go out with my dear husband once a week. I do not smoke, I do not play cards, and strong drinks do not appeal to me. My mother-in-law, however, likes all these things.

I keep my home in good order. I like every corner to be clean and everything in place. I get up early and begin immediately to clean the house, then I get dressed. Even at home, I like to be dressed like a lady.

My mother-in-law likes to sleep late, and the moment she gets up she has a cigarette in her mouth. And wherever one turns, one sees the ashes and cigarette stubs. She never makes her bed and her room is always a mess. She doesn't get dressed but sits down in her bathrobe, with her black coffee, by the television set. Later, she begins to phone her friends to plan where to meet them. She goes with them to the beauty parlor (she recently turned from a brunette to a blonde), another day they go hunting for bargains in the department stores, she runs to cocktail parties, and she plays cards till late at night.

Lately she has started bringing her group of cardplayers to my home and this I cannot stand. Besides the fact that I can't condone their wasting so much time at cards, I have to spend several days cleaning up after them.

I don't want to hurt my dear husband, and so far I haven't

spoken to him about this. And I don't want an argument with my mother-in-law. I don't say a word to her because everyone has a right to lead her life as she pleases. But something must be done and I ask your advice.

Respectfully,
The Old-Fashioned Daughter-in-law

ANSWER:
When we read your letter, it really seemed to us that you and your mother-in-law had changed roles. Usually a mother-in-law has these complaints about her daughter-in-law. In your case it's just the opposite.

We feel that the fairest way to solve the problem is for your mother-in-law to move out and make a home for herself. If she wants to be near you and your child, she can live in the neighborhood. She is still a young woman and should not have given up her own home. Since she knew well that you conduct your life so differently from hers, she should understand that you could not live together for long. Talk this over with your husband first, and then you should both explain warmly and kindly to your mother-in-law why it is not practical for her to live with you.

1967

Dear Editor,

I have often read the "Bintel Brief" to learn how you have suggested solutions for the problems of your readers. Now, I would like to tell you my problem. It is difficult for me to write Yiddish so I am writing to you in English. I am a young man twenty years of age. My grandparents brought a precious heritage of *Yiddishkeit* from Eastern Europe. I remember the good Jewish life they lived. I still remember how they used to sing Jewish songs, speak Yiddish, and prepare delicious *kosher* meals for my parents and me on Friday evenings. These were the best days I have yet known.

However, several years ago my grandparents passed away. My parents and I now reside in the suburbs in an area which lacks the Jewish traditions and customs that I knew as a child. Very few except the older Jewish people in my neighborhood speak Yiddish. Few keep strictly *kosher* homes, few people observe our wonderful Sabbath in the traditional manner. Most of the young ladies I meet are not the type of Jewish girl I would like. I feel like a stranger among the Jewish girls who are interested only in rock 'n' roll and wear mini skirts. I long for the days I knew as a young boy.

Many aspects of life in this area seem to snuff out whatever remains of our beloved *Yiddishkeit*. I have recently graduated from a local university and am now starting to attend law school in a larger city. Most of the young people who will be studying there with me will not be Jewish or will be the type of Jew who does not live as one. Most of the people I will come in contact with will not have the same interests I have.

I want to know how my family and I can perpetuate our traditions. I would also like to know where I can find people of my age to share my interests.

Sincerely,
S.T.

ANSWER:

Blessed be the grandmothers and grandfathers who brought with them to this country the spiritual values of generations deeply rooted in Jewish life. A great many of their American children and grandchildren did not show any interest in upholding and continuing this rich, spiritual heritage. That you do not now have the Jewish atmosphere you long for is in great part the fault of your parents because they did not carry on in the same tradition of your grandparents. Had they brought you up in the traditions of your grandfather, you would now have a circle of friends in which you could live as you desire.

The atmosphere, the life to which you are drawn, is usually not found in the suburbs. But if you were to come New York to study, you could find a circle of young people and the environment you long for.

Thus the "Bintel Brief."

Thus the history of the Jewish immigrants to the United States who settled on the Lower East Side of New York.

One thing we learn from the "Bintel Brief" is that the Jewish immigrants were optimistic. Despite the struggle to earn a living, the trials and tribulations of learning the language of a new country and social prejudice, there was optimism.

My own early morning impression of the East Side, and I mean six o'clock in the morning, summer and winter, was of young boys streaming out of tenements to go to the synagogue to say a prayer for a departed parent before going to school, and maybe also carrying up a fifty-pound bag of coal before breakfast. Work, work, work.

Everybody worked all the time, and if there was no job, people worked at something; they sorted rags or sewed garments or fixed flowers and feathers for hat manufacturers. People scrabbled for a little living. They did anything for the children. They wanted their children to enter the American middle class. "My son will be a doctor," they'd say, "or a lawyer, maybe a teacher." I never heard anyone express lesser hopes for his child.

Who has ever seen such optimism anywhere on earth? A man peddled fourteen hours, maybe, and brought home two dollars after he paid off his merchandise and his cart hire, or he brought home eleven dollars a week from the factory for fifty-four hours' work. But at night the sweatshop employees, men and women who sat at machines for nine and ten hours a day, came home, washed up, had supper and went to the lodge hall or settlement houses to learn English or to listen to a fellow read poetry to them. Paid readers of poetry! I saw it. I saw gangsters and bums—the ones the fiction fakers write about—but I also saw poets, settlement workers, welfare workers, scribes, teachers, philosophers, all hoping, and striving for one goal—to break away from their disad-

*vantaged lives—and they did, too. The second generation came
along and soon the sons took the old folks away, out to Brooklyn
or up to the Bronx, and thus they made room for new immigrants.
America gave them all hope and life, and they repaid America.
There has never been a more even trade.*

GLOSSARY

Alef-Beis	Jewish alphabet
Bar Mitzvah	confirmation of boy at thirteen
Bris	circumcision ceremony
Chutzpa	impudence, nerve
Elul	twelfth month in the Jewish calendar
Galitzianer	native of Galicia
Gemore	part of the Talmud
Kaddish	prayer said by mourners
Kheyder	elementary religious Jewish school
Kohen	descendant of the ancient Jewish priests
Kosher, kashruth	Jewish dietary laws .
Landsleit	countrymen
Minyan	the ten men required for a Jewish religious service
Rebbe	Hasidic rabbi
Rosh Hashanah	the Jewish New Year
Schnapps	brandy, whiskey
Shadkhan	matchmaker
Shikse	Gentile girl
Shive	the seven days of mourning
Shokhet	Jewish ritual slaughterer
Shtetel	small town
Shul	synagogue
Talmud Torah	elementary religious Hebrew school
Torah	the five books of Moses, also the entire body of teaching, Old Testament and Talmud
Yeshiva	Talmudic school
Yom Kippur	the Day of Atonement
Yohrzeit	annual observance for the dead
Yiddishkeit	Jewishness